Positively
THE LAST WORD ON
EXMOOR

Best Wishes

Norma Huxtable

Exmoor 2004

Positively

THE LAST WORD ON
EXMOOR

NORMA HUXTABLE

HALSGROVE

First published in Great Britain in 2002
Copyright © 2002 Norma Huxtable

ISBN 1 84114 177 1

British Library Cataloguing-in-Publication Data
A CIP record for this title is available from the British Library

HALSGROVE
Halsgrove House
Lower Moor Way
Tiverton, Devon EX16 6SS
Tel: 01884 243242
Fax: 01884 243325
email sales@halsgrove.com
website www.halsgrove.com

Printed and bound in Great Britain by
The Cromwell Press, Trowbridge

Winter Warmers

Winter is my least favourite time of year. As I get older, each winter seems colder and more austere. If it were not for living on Exmoor and the socialising that is part and parcel of the countryside, I would opt to curl up and hibernate, to be brought back to life by the birds singing on a warm spring day and the heady scent of primroses over all. That is dreaming, and there is no room for that sort of nonsense in a busy farm schedule. As for waking to the sound of the dawn chorus, you can do that any spring morning and paradoxically all I feel is murderous at having my sleep interrupted, only too aware that the next voice I hear in the dawn chorus pattern will be the F/H/B intoning, 'Git yer boots on, Maid.'

From this you can tell the winter is not exactly my favourite time, and here I am not alone, as the animals don't go much on it either. The pigs always look pale and peaky, the chickens decide laying eggs is too draughty a job, and even the five ginger farm cats drop out and sign on the dole round the kitchen Rayburn. But the socialising makes up for much of the gloom of the short, dark days – there are always parties in friends' houses, and card schools and whist drives, and, best of all village dances. Our old pig wagon would transport us grudgingly round the countryside, and, no matter how seedy the weather or how ill-tempered the engine, nine times out of ten we would, eventually, wheeze up to our destination. Getting started was the first obstacle to be surmounted, and I've lost count of the times the F/H/B's freezing face would appear at the kitchen window with his mouth opening and shutting and his words whipped away by the wind. I heard not a single word, but in seconds I would be dragging on boots and mac, because I would know I was wanted on a matter of some urgency. I would like to put this down to rapport between husband and wife, but sadly it had nothing to do with rapport, it was more a matter of constant repetition, more like the pig wagon's refusal to start, nearly always in pouring rain and a force ten gale. The pig wagon would be hitched to the tractor and dragged for a considerable distance down the road, with one of us driving each vehicle. I grumbled that I was allocated the tractor when it was pouring with rain (there was no cab then) but the F/H/B always said mysteriously, it was better that way. Many a time my boot slipped off the clutch and I would be away to a flying start as the tow rope parted in the middle and I would look round in the dark (there were no lights on the tractor) to glimpse the F/H/B in the pig wagon, jumping up and down like he was sitting on a tin-tack, with his mouth opening and shutting like a machine gun rat-tatting, but, mercifully, the roar of the tractor would drown his words.

After a chilly half-mile, the rehitched vehicle usually managed to start, then it was all stations go to get changed and back into our chariot for our night out. Racing through the kitchen to change we would pass the ginger cats purring happily in the warmth, a sight which seemed to incense the F/H/B who reckoned never to carry passengers, and he would seize the nearest broom and attempt to sweep them out through the back door, whilst I sloshed milk into their pie-dish and encouraged them to stay in the warm. More often than not our evening got off to a shaky start. Standing in the bedroom without my corduroys and indestructible socks I would feel like a chicken stripped of its feathers, and I often wished a fancy trouser suit might fulfil any aspirations for both warmth and a smidgeon of glamour, but the F/H/B reckoned that even if I got my sturdy legs in, my behind would be like trying to squeeze a hundredweight of corn into a half-hundredweight sack. He compensated, kindly saying that if he'd wanted a glamour-pants then he wouldn't have married me, would he? I could always rummage round the back of the wardrobe and dig out my old creaseproof crimplene, whilst consoling myself that I was never noticeable when grouped together with the other farmers' wives as we assumed a sort of mass uniformity, with our broad backs and rippling muscles, more like boxers ready for the Big Fight than ladies about to trip the Dinkyone-Step. And of course the F/H/B was quite right when he said, 'What h'odds about fashion so long's a maid looks respectable.'

At the dance I mingled with the other boxers in the Paul Jones, and round and round we circled, and when the music stopped, nine times out of ten, I ended up facing a wooden plaque on the wall that sternly insisted, 'Play up and play the game', and out of the corner of my eye I always spotted the F/H/B, all five foot of him and well out of my reach, dive in to emerge waltzing gaily with a six-foot film star dressed in a gold trouser suit with a bare midriff. I had never felt older or uglier, or, worst of all, more respectable, so I did not mind sitting out sipping my Babycham, with a familiar figure bearing down on me. 'Twas Seemingly. Too late I would realise he was cidered-up, as the two of us wobbled across the floor, arms pumping for dear life, to the strains of 'Strangers in the night', Seemingly's glazed eyes not focusing anywhere in particular. I would prop him up and steer hard around and he would lean alarmingly towards me to deliver a saucy little compliment. 'Missus,' he would say admiringly, 'you be as strong as a horse. Seemingly so!'

There was likely to be a free-for-all in the Lancers, and in the Grand March I would endeavour to score a bullseye with my heel on the F/H/B's toe, but he would be having such a good time he obviously wouldn't feel it, whirling and twirling like a mad dervish.

At the end of the evening (carriages at 1am) the wives would collect their farmers from the opposite end of the bar and the F/H/B offered Seemingly a lift home in our pig wagon. He would collapse happily into the passenger seat and start to snore, whilst we loaded his pushbike into the back and I hauled up my skirt and climbed in beside it. The F/H/B would look at the sky and reckon "tis going to snow' and our sheep ought to be removed to more sheltered ground.

'Soon's us git home, Maid,' he would say, 'git your boots on!'

The winter weather on Exmoor often merges into a pot-pourri of cloud, drizzle and fog but thankfully the mood rarely matches the climate. Far from taking the opportunity to put their feet up, Exmoor folk take off out-and-about or 'urnabout' as it is termed. Parties, card schools and slide shows unfailingly draw the revellers, every event followed by a gargantuan supper, the belief being that no evening should be conducted with empty innards. Exmoor, like armies, marches on its stomach.

On winter evenings the moors are alive with carloads of card players in search of whist drives. They select their venue before they set off from the cosy comfort of their warm homes for a chilly hall, but it can be hit or miss whether they ever reach their selected village hall in the fog. The crammed-in passengers all shout different directions, though given the number of whist drives on any one night, any place will do such is their enthusiasm, even if they end up sitting freezing in their overcoats and woolly hats. Once settled the evening commences with an exchange of friendly greetings as it's near enough always the same faces, different place, a bit like a big party always on the move. Some play cards with the traditional poker face; others try gamesmanship scooping up their cards with a despairing aside, 'This hand's as black as a cow's innards', aware that bull can often baffle brains. The F/H/B always reckons that hearing the first shout of 'Hearts is trumps' very nearly ties with the huntsman blowing 'Gone away' in his list of favourite things. Everybody in the hall hears Granny Pugsley cough loudly, which is Granny's signal to her partner that she's holding the ace of trumps. At table number ten a twelve-year-old shuffles the pack with the expertise of a New Orleans card sharp, and any newcomer, marvelling at such skill is told matter-of-factly by the young player, 'Well, I've had twelve years of experience!' He knows the score, having been brought up on 'carding' ever since he can remember, like most country kids.

There are two players left over, so this means sitting out for one deal at a 'flirtation' table, where they each take a generous eight points. The flirtation is not of the lonely hearts type, the conversation likely to be revolving round udder cream and worm drench.

Neighbourliness and old-world courtesy may take a downturn in the second half when a couple of points can make the difference between taking home a full-blown chicken dinner or a tin of 'super-saver' baked beans. Here a hesitant player can earn a scornful rebuke for ruining a partner's hand by placing a low card instead of a high one – 'tis no good sending a boy to do a man's work!'

Prizes abound and even for the lowest score there is what used to be called the booby, now renamed more kindly, the consolation prize, upgraded some say, by human rights' campaigners refusing to acknowledge the degrading 'booby'. For the losers, there's still a chance in the raffle, with another chicken dinner, whisky, wine, a home-made fruit cake – all high-grade prizes, but no baked beans in this one. That would be lowering the standard. After a supper of ham sandwiches and fruit cake we all pile into our transport and disappear into the fog; for some (non-prize winners) it's been a standard night out, for others (winners) a fantastic night. Those are the only two sorts of night you get at whist drives. They all tell you – there's no such thing as a bad one.

◇◇◆◇◇

On Exmoor we always say that Christmas starts on 1 December and finishes on 1 March, which just about encapsulates it. Well, nearly, because it gets earlier every year, and it might be nearer the truth to say Christmas starts some time in November, and fizzles out towards the middle of March, when the early-birds commence lambing, the main lambing commencing on 1 April when there is likely to be some grass about.

The Christmas pig has always been an institution, being fattened for months on the best of everything and ready to be slaughtered in good time for the festivities. The pig is now, in modern times, transported to the nearest abattoir, whereas in years past it was a marathon operation undertaken at home as an all-day job when the pork was salted and stored in large dome containers called psalters, and never to be touched by a woman with her period as the meat would not keep. This worked very well so long as there was an R in the month because nobody ever slaughtered in the summer months; every bit of the pig was usable, except, they used to say, the tail and the squeak. And the whole family found the feasting irresistible, from the baby in its pram trying its teeth on lightly fried fat bacon to Granfer in his nineties packing away his breakfast of fat bacon with fried bread, egg, potatoes and laver, a greenish-black seaweed speciality picked off the North Devon coast. The presentation of these delicacies had much the same effect on the uninitiated as a dishful of sheep's eyes in Saudi Arabia. Any leftovers went straight into the pigs' bucket under the sink for recycling, and the same bucket came in handy for emergencies with less robust gourmets. Roast pork would follow for midday dinner, the first joint to be eaten being the 'sticking joint' which was the neck where the pig's throat was slit, and which would never keep, not even in the psalter. The biggest treats came at teatime, when little 'frying pieces', or chitlings as they were called, were sliced off the pig's intestines and served fried in dripping with hunks of dry bread to mop up the juices. It was a busy time for the farmer's wife and daughters, as there was 'potten pudding' to be made, encased in the washed-out intestines, which over the years has become hogs pudding, and some folk, but not many, made black puddings from the blood. The trotters could be roasted, with leeks, but were very fatty – and delicious brawn was made from the head, set in its own jelly which was the liquid the head was cooked in reduced by boiling and poured over the chopped up meat to set in a cool dairy. I remember breaking the golden rule, once, which was never to get friendly with a pig you intend to eat. He was such an engaging little chap; we became buddies and I reared him and fattened him, until the inevitable happened and he went for slaughter for our own use. I steeled myself to do all the necessary packaging up, but the F/H/B wanted his brawn and into the pot went the head with onions, carrots and bay leaves. I slammed the lid on the big saucepan, but had to remove it after a couple of hours to top up the liquid, and there was my little friend's head looking up at me. It was one of the most traumatic experiences of my life. I made the brawn, shedding salt tears over it, but I did not eat it, neither have I made it or eaten it since.

Now pigs are transported for slaughter to the nearest abattoir and anybody who daydreams that any idiot can load a pig soon realises that plans have to be made. For a start, vehicles have to be pig-proofed, then men have to be mustered and neighbours within a couple of miles warned to expect ear-splitting shrieks from both men and pig. Small, home-made trailers can be time-wasters when all four sides collapse as the pig takes up residence, and with the carpenter wishing he'd never been born. The F/H/B once set off with a large pig in the trailer, and all seemed to be going like clockwork until he stopped to pass the time of day with an elderly retired farmer friend who wanted to know where he was off to towing a trailer. The F/H/B jerked his thumb backwards, saying he was on his way to the slaughterhouse at Tiverton with the Christmas pig, whereupon the retired gentleman smoothed his moustache, peered into the trailer, straightened and thoughtfully admonished, 'Well, me lad, you might be going to the slaughterhouse, but you ain't got no pig.' Disbelieving, the F/H/B checked on the trailer, only to find his passenger had jumped ship somewhere back along the route. There was no pig. He hurriedly reversed, thanking his lucky stars that he had stopped to have a word with his old friend, before turning up pigless in Tiverton and suffering the jeering humiliation the slaughterman would have heaped on him. The two of them then set back up the road to Chilcott, and there, no more than half a mile from home, was the fat pig, casually munching grass by the roadside, which they then managed to bundle back into the trailer and the rest of the journey was concluded.

The advent of freezers revolutionised pig keeping, although it was essential to have mains electricity in place of the old generators, while some farms to this day still do not have Mains, the cost being phenomenal. Many an engine is tied together with baling cord by those optimists who still naively believe the forgotten promises of the electricity board to electrify every house on the moor. It is not surprising that folks even say that sound travels faster than light in these parts with so many pubs, cottages and farms powered by ancient generators. Swapping these for Mains could be like swapping an old rusty bicycle for a Ferrari. Possibly a number of folk could sink into unfit slothfulness merely flicking a switch on the wall, when at present they are reasonably athletic ministering to a generator often situated as ours once was, across a small muddy field arranged like an army assault course, with recumbent pigs, piles of logs, cow-pats and sheets of galvanised to navigate, in a small oil-spattered shed known rather grandly as the Engine House. It presented a challenge to all of us womenfolk who were expected to master the complexities of the starting system of a wilful 1hp motor, which involved petrol, paraffin and water, and, worst of all, a massive starting handle, separate from the machine itself, which had to be fitted on and then swung at speed and whipped off before the whole caboosh spluttered into life, otherwise it could have soared straight through the roof. Or killed the operator. Or both. The only two extras after the grudging light that our engine allowed were the milking machine and television. But not both at once. The TV was less than perfect, the actors being transformed into unrecognisable little fat cowboys on fat, hairy horses, whilst corpulent male ballet dancers hoisted tubby ballerinas in the air surrounded by a roly-poly corps de ballet in tutus lumbering through Swan Lake. On a winter's evening, after milking, the F/H/B would set the engine up to supply us in the house with lights and TV for the next two or three hours. At around 8.30 came the deadline for a refill of paraffin and water, otherwise the lights dimmed drastically and the TV picture shrank to a one-inch square. We both used to watch the hands on the clock creep past eight, and then the argument would start, usually with the F/H/B commencing, 'Your turn, Maid, to see to the engine. I done it last night,' and my reply, 'I don't want to see football anyway.' Then from the distance, the sound of the engine put-putting as it slowed down and the rush to the back door, the boots, the freezing-cold run across the field to save it before it all petered into a sullen silence, albeit still viciously steaming, and hissing. I remember one dark night throwing myself through the door and touching a live wire with my knee, which heaved me straight out the door again into the pig's muck heap. And every night the whole operation had to be repeated for a third time to turn off the engine. Sometimes if we had neighbours into supper the F/H/B would instruct as they left, 'Somebody turn off the engine when you go past.' It mattered not that nobody would actually be going past, but by the time they had left the F/H/B would have done a miraculous quick change into his striped pyjamas saying, 'Come on, Maid, git that motor turned off.' Then it would be into my boots and off across the small exposed muddy field to turn off the paraffin and a race back to the house as the motor put-putted down, undoing my pinny and unbuttoning buttons and falling into the house as the lights dimmed and it was all over and out. Barring accidents, which were inevitable from time to time, I was spurred on to break my own records; the F/H/B, timed me once and I completed the whole exercise in two and a half minutes.

Although I always looked on our generator as a demanding monster, I know many are regarded as part of the family, and are even given names such as Jim or Jaws or Bonzo, with their little sheds referred to as Jim's House, and so on. The doors usually remain open for flying entrances (and exits). 'Quick Jim's starving, he wants water/petrol/paraffin.' Or even 'Jim's constipated', a blockage surgically dealt with by a swipe with a hammer across Jim's vitals.

The engine house was a mecca for roosting hens and even cats seeking a maternity ward, deafening, but invitingly warm and even hotter when it caught fire, on average about twice a year. Seemingly still reminisces about the night his old engine backfired and a sheet of flame precipitated him out through the door, his stringy old frame lightly covered in soot, leaving only the whites of his eyes showing and with the backside of his breeches on fire. Luckily the water trough was handy and he promptly sat in it and dowsed the flames.

The Rolls-Royce of engines is a Start-o-matic, which we never aspired to; luckily, the Mains came our way. Next to the Mains, the Start-o-matic is the ultimate device, doing away with the tyranny of the starting handle, and operating at the flick of a switch, any switch, anywhere, without going anywhere near the engine house. With a

Start-o-matic a countrywoman can throw out her dolly board and enjoy the luxury of a washing machine, just so long as she never clashes with the cows and their milking machines. She can hoover, though not at the same time as the infra-red lamps are on in the pig houses. And she can even invest in a small freezer, so long as she remembers to switch off at sheep-shearing time. But there is light to go to bed by, though not to switch on in the middle of the night, because that kicks the whole works into action. And then there is the gadget that challenges all gadgets: the Master Switch. The three brothers who lived in Chilcott before us were Uncle Henry, Uncle Percy and Uncle Fred. Uncle Henry, being the eldest, was in charge and over Uncle Henry's bed was the Master Switch for their Start-o-matic. Not only did it provide electricity for the farmhouse, but for an additional two cottages. One was next door, the other some distance away across the fields. And when Uncle Henry retired for the night, he would settle comfortably into his bed, read the newspaper, then his thumb would go upwards and hover over the Master Switch before plunging all three properties into darkness. It could be early or late, depending on Uncle Henry's constitution on the day or, as some of the unhappy cottage dwellers were inclined to remark, pure and simple bloody-mindedness. It was never consistent, more of a cliff-hanger, and not exactly geared for good neighbourly relations. If Uncle Henry decided on an early night and the cottagers were watching a play on TV there would be no warning, just darkness and a suddenly blank screen. It must be said we never really appreciated the comedy of our old TV until we were on the Mains, and the dancers and the cowboys slimmed down, and the summer-holiday programmes from Mediterranean climes, which had nearly always been viewed through heavy snowstorms, suddenly looked warmly inviting. But nothing seemed as funny anymore. We scarcely recognised our own Prime Minister who seemed to shed three stone overnight, and lady actresses, with what the F/H/B observed admiringly to be 'backsides like stallions' metamorphosed into 'all teeth and scrag-end, like skintered cows'.

There's no pleasing some folks…

Some say it seems like Christmas all the year round on Exmoor, but that cannot be, and that is why it is slotted in between December 1st and March 1st. Parties abound, and whilst the rest of England mingles,

Exmoor goes 'urnabout. Slide shows are popular, even with only two subjects on hand – one the wild red deer and the other foxhunting. Card schools with keen gamblers carry on in private homes across the moor, accompanied by copious amounts of food and drink. I was sitting next to one local worthy at a party when he confessed to being 'a bit under the weather, Maid'. He went on to tell me he had been out for thirty-six nights on the trot – 'Me head knowed I had to git outa bed but me legs wouldn't hold up.' And with more to come, he felt he was flagging a bit that morning. What about his Missus, I wondered. 'Oh, I lefted her there – got me own breakfast.'

'You still managed breakfast then?'

'Well you know what it is, Maid, not a lot – a pinta cider and a cream cracker.' What a big-hearted man, I thought, to leave his Missus in bed – it doesn't often happen that way. Maybe it's because the Exmoor male actually does believe his Missus has a tough job.

◇◇◆◇◇

Many visitors turn up year after year and even make special journeys to the West Country in the winter to join in parties and fund-raising events, usually saying they have nothing like it in towns. It is telling that some holidaymakers declare they know more people on Exmoor than in their own street. It is unlikely that any of those present at the cheese and wine party at our place in 1987 has ever forgotten it. Some cheese and wine parties have a theme, or a competition for a bit of added interest, a quiz or everyone dressed as vicars and tarts, not that this is ever a necessity, with everyone so pleased to see one another that there is a buzz of non-stop conversation. And with a lot of countrymen despising the wine bottle, it can turn into more of a cheese and whisky party. But in 1987 the cheese and wine/whisky took place at Chilcott, and the added interest was a contest to pick Miss Dung Heap 1987 – for men only. There were only seven brave contestants one being the F/H/B in a dress (not in a rig-out run-up by me, I'd sooner skin a rabbit than pick up a needle and cotton), topped with a bonnet tied under his chin. He had a thing about bonnets, mainly because he had a face bonnets suited. He once won a baby contest wearing rompers and a pink bonnet (he was fifty-four at the time), his pram being pushed by our huntsman dressed as a nanny. But the title of Miss Dung Heap eluded him. The winner, picked by independent judges, was a beefy 6ft tall farmer sporting a bubbly ginger wig and squeezed into his mother's old green evening dress, his naily boots peeping from under the figure hugging skirt. The six losers jeered their disapproval at the judges' (impartial) verdict, the one in a be-ribboned red hat mouthing 'ratbag' at the winner who, uncaring and jubilant, was already slurping from his first-prize bottle of whisky. As this was fifteen years ago, the phrase 'men in drag' summed it up, conjuring up visions of Les Dawson lookalike guys in skirts and stays parodying hairy-chested women straight out of the sheep dip. Nowadays 'drag' is not such a laughing matter as it is important for men to be (quote), 'In touch with their feminine side', turning HE into SHE at the flick of a dominant wife's little finger, and even strutting their stuff in the street wearing her sarong ('underwear and all, dearie!'). This 'new man' as he's called is even rumoured to watch his weight, picking at a wholemeal sandwich filled with finely chopped parsley for his lunch, and would probably throw up at the sight of our old knackerman skinning a well-ripened dead sheep then wiping his knife on the backside of his dirt-stiffened corduroy breeches before slicing up his lunch of fat bacon wedged in thick slices of white bread. Then washing it all down with a bottle of cold tea (no milk) and closing the repast with a slurp from a muddied hip flask. At about the same time as the 'new man' is in the Met bar twining bejewelled fingers around his first Margarita cocktail of the day. What the F/H/B always called a black dog for a monkey, whatever that means, but somehow it sounds about right. Pontificating, I suppose – but then, most farmers pontificate – and do you know, they've usually got it spot on right, so it's pointless arguing.

Another old winter favourite with the country community is the quiz. The quizzes, usually in a village hall (with a licence), or pub, holds great attractions for vast numbers of teams on a knockout basis, with a few participants thinking to air their general knowledge and the majority lured into attending to partake at the bar. One local lady left brooding at home after backing out on her team, then regretting it, decided after a couple of inspirational G & Ts to go along anyway just to liven things up a bit. She selected her long crimson dress, in itself a red light to those who knew her – topped it with a curly orange wig and sallied along to the venue. 'I decided I'd go as Natasha Shagnasty, the beautiful Russian spy,' she recounted to a crowd of us at a meeting the next day. 'I was a bit late and they were all having supper when I arrived, so I sailed straight up to the bar and ordered a treble G & T. I spotted lots of friends and waved my ostrich-feather boa in their direction, and the landlord wasn't looking very happy, so I flicked him with it as well, and I s'pose all in all, I was causing a bit of a commotion, but that's why I went didn't I? The next thing is his Lordship's leaning over the bar and hissing – yes, hissing, at me, "I must ask you to go. Please leave. Go now, and go quietly."' At this Natasha Shagnasty drew herself up to her imposing full height, pressing her colourfully made up face against his, her orange curls bobbing with indignation. 'I said to him in my best county voice, "You silly little man, surely you recognise me? I hunt with your hounds!"' She was backed up by a voice at her elbow belonging to the Secretary of the Tiverton Foxhounds who had incredibly recognised the colourful Natasha.

'She's who she says she is,' said her rescuer.

'I can vouch for her. I'm her pimp!'

By the time the glorious Natasha had finished recounting her tale, we were all wiping the tears from our eyes. 'Oh,' I exclaimed, 'I wish I'd been there to see you!'

'If I'd known that, old thing,' she said, 'I'd have picked you up. You could have come as my cousin Titiana Pissoffski.'

'Next time,' I told her, 'next time, Natasha.'

The F/H/B and I had never been invited to appear together in a quiz, the way some knowledgeable folk are in demand and this made us only too aware that we hardly presented a fearsome combination to any competing teams. Therefore, we were more than flattered to both be invited to take part in a competition at Dulverton Town Hall, known as Mr & Mrs. We were told this was a popular TV quiz show, although neither of us had ever seen it, so it had to be explained to us in detail. As the name indicated, Mr & Mrs was a husband-and-wife partnership in competition with other couples. Each partner was to be interviewed individually by a quizmaster, with the same questions being asked of each. The winners would be the couple that responded with matching answers. The six couples competing would be a cross-section of the community, including ourselves as the only farming couple, our local policeman and his wife, and the youngest couple who were newlyweds.

The event was to be staged on a Saturday evening at seven o'clock and we had a few guests staying at the time, so I had to press them into having an early dinner. We were still using our downstairs bedroom, the one we called our 'summer' room, north facing, cool, and with great hooks hanging from the ceiling. A smallish window opened out onto the side garden, which, despite the coolness, we usually kept open. On the quiz night I hurriedly changed, sprayed myself lavishly with perfume, laid out the F/H/B's clothes on the bed for that night, and returned to the kitchen to clear up as far as possible. The F/H/B changed in record time – he always did – and turned up neat and tidy and ready, but with a face like thunder. 'Maid,' he said, 'that bleddy old Tom cat's bin in our room and the place is stinking. He must 'ave come in through the window.' Oh no, I thought, fearing for the tatty old tabby wild cat that I had encouraged by feeding him daily outside. I had even named him Satchmo, because of his deep, warbling voice. I had to admit he was not only decrepit, but untrustworthy, and I hoped he was not hiding under the bed, but thought I had better check as the F/H/B's wrath was something to behold, and I was taking all the stick for it. Back in the bedroom I found my fears misplaced, as there was, indeed, a very strong whiff about the place, but I immediately recognised it as the perfume I had earlier sprayed over myself. I was jubilant to relay this information to the F/H/B who hated to be wrong about anything and huffed and puffed that if I would spray myself with rubbish that 'stinked like tom-cats' pee', then anybody could make a mistake, with a final 'If I catch that dirty bugger in our room I'll shoot it.' I tried to explain that my scent was not rubbish but Elizabeth Arden's Blue Grass, but explanations were brushed aside as we set off, not speaking, to try to win our happy marriage Mr & Mrs Competition.

The Town Hall was a-buzz, with light, music, and a full house, everyone expecting their money's worth after parting with 50p a ticket. Full of trepidation, with the five other couples, who all appeared professional actors, such was their aplomb, we were all hustled on stage and given our last-minute instructions. The curtains parted to tumultuous applause, and we were 'on'. The policeman and his wife were the first couple to be introduced to the audience, the M.C. dwelling on the wife on account of her work at the Minehead Cottage Hospital as, she was, what he called 'a scrubber', which set the tone for the evening, much to the delight of the fee-paying public. The M.C. has always been a gift to Exmoor with his smooth, groomed, articulate performance, a chap with a very quick turn of wit, one Les Silverlock. He has no compunction whatsoever about dropping people – be it in sporting events or after-dinner speeches – right in what the F/H/B likes to call Shitters' Ditch and this serves to enhance his popularity and pull in the crowds. The contest was won by the couple who had been married for nearly three weeks, and we were last, not surprisingly after our earlier run-in with the cat.

That night, as an added interest, the compère informed the audience – and us, it being the first we'd heard of it – that the lady contestants would be lined up on stage, and each of the husbands would, in turn, be blindfolded and allocated five seconds per female for 'feelies', the winner being the husband who identified his own wife. This brought the house down, excitement mounting as the blindfolded contestants nervously approached each lady. The local policeman ran his hands over me then triumphantly picked me for his own wife, which did nothing to further anybody's confidence in his detective powers, particularly as she was a foot taller than me. Only one got it right – my F/H/B. 'Weren't you the clever one,' I crowed afterwards, old scores and resentment forgotten, wiped out by this magnificent victory.

'Easy,' he said modestly. 'You wuz the only one that stinked of tom-cats' pee.'

'That was scent.'

'You call it what you like and I'll call it what I likes.'

Hand-in-glove with every event in the country (and probably in towns too) go the raffles, essential money-spinners the whole caboosh often resting on glittering prizes donated, the F/H/B calls it 'scrounged' from friends and neighbours. But how sad that so few win the prize they really want. The F/H/B once won a trip in a helicopter from South Molton, but he suffers from vertigo and gave it away to one of our visitors (as it was on a Sunday afternoon, I could not use it, having to be at home cooking dinner for the guests). Then, another time, I was thrilled when the F/H/B won a candlelit dinner for two with a glass of wine in the local bistro. He was less than pleased and tried to swap it with the second prizewinner who had collected bags of coal given by the local fuel merchant. The F/H/B was not unduly surprised when the winner of the coal decided to keep it. 'I'd hev done the same meself,' he said, 'us'll just hev to make the best of a bad job!' He vowed not to collect his candlelit dinner for two – 'Not likely, Maid, you and me sat there with half Exmoor looking at us munching a bit of rice on a lettuce leaf!' Eventually we booked in but took half a dozen neighbours with us. An even more sophisticated raffle followed, offering a weekend in Paris to the winner. Tickets were sold in their thousands, everybody was after that weekend in Paris. Except the wife of the man who won. 'I don't want to go to thik old place,' she cried, 'I'd sooner have a weekend in Bournemouth' – which is just where she changed it for. One of my guests, a vegetarian, told of the time when she won a 30lb turkey in a raffle, then had to hire a taxi to take her and the unwanted bird home. Why, you may ask, do folk spend money on draw tickets offering unsuitable prizes? It's because they never expect to win, and, more worthily, feel they are contributing to a good cause. If they win one of the minor prizes, way down the list, they are often delighted. I remember my sister-in-law Stella winning a blue satin-covered coat-hanger and bearing it triumphantly home, waving it over her head like it was – a winning lottery ticket.

◇◇◆◇◇

Winter (2)
Visitors and Valentines

Cow punchers in the Wild West are said to commence their day shovelling down a breakfast of kick-arse cornflakes with milk poured over from a bottle labelled Jack Daniels. The F/H/B has always opted for a healthier breakfast of fat bacon, fried eggs, fried bread, fried heeltaps (King Edwards) and, when available laver, the black seaweed gathered from the North Devon coast. If the contents of the plate look a bit thin, then a couple of lamb chops are often added. The size of this breakfast usually eliminates the necessity of keeping body and soul together with 'forenoons!', alias elevenses, a must-have in days past. That was before farmers and their wives concerned themselves about looking like their own pigs wearing jumpers. With no forenoons to boost their intake, the men folk are good and ready for their dinner at one o'clock sharp. Whilst the rest of England lunches, country folk sit round kitchen tables to gravy dinners, roasts and stews and cow pie, presided over by Missus in her floral pinny. Her job is to dish up dinner on time; there is absolutely no question of her not being present to wait on the menfolk, although she is never included in their conversation, other than, 'Over this way with the tetties, Maid.'

Farmer, sitting at the head of the table, eats as much as he can for a man with only one mouth, siphoning in food like a tractor taking on fuel, firm in the belief that no decision, no matter how piddling, should ever be made on an empty stomach. Mountainous puddings, smothered in clotted cream, are expertly dealt with before they go back to work, fortified, ready and raring to confront any dissenters, from marauding tax-men to anti-country sports agitators who have possibly lunched less courageously on half a sandwich filled with finely chopped herbs and washed down with turnip juice. After lunch, I sometimes catch a glimpse through the window of the small army of men out in the yard, then sigh heavily before turning to tackle the pile of dirty dishes, with the unworthy thought that as far as I'm concerned a man at the sink has got to be worth two in the yard.

Although countrymen can hardly be classed a fussy eaters, a few taboos from Granddad's day still prevail. Blackberries are never picked after 29 September when the devil spits on them. Seemingly, never known for his culinary art, reckons the only way to cook a wild goose is with a brick in the oven, then after a couple of days slow roasting, he throws out the goose and slices up the brick and serves it with gravy. Seemingly, the F/H/B and most other sheep farmers have curiously delicate innards and spurn mutton and red jelly at lambing time.

The eating habits of immigrants to Exmoor are observed and often learnt from, although at times they emphasise the culinary gap between town and country. Our neighbours, Patricia and Richard, who retired to a nearby cottage from London, talked in aristocratic voices knowledgeably of their many lunches at the Ritz, and nouvelle cuisine. She was a tall, good-looking, stick-thin lady who wore big hats to stunning effect, and whose whole life centred round fashion and beauty and booze, or aperitifs, as she called it – and people with titles; emitting regularly phrases such as 'I was only saying to Sir George last week... when he interrupted in that charming way he has, and said, "Oh, no, Patricia, dear, please, not Sir George, you really must call me Loopy!" So now I do and next week Loopy is taking us to the races... Do you know Sir George?' This was rhetorical because if I do, which is very unlikely, she is careful to say Sir George, because in her book she would never have expected a peer of the realm to know a working farmer. She would have been mortified if he had instructed me and the F/H/B to, 'Call me Loopy'. In fact in days to come Loopy regularly got an airing in the conversation. Patricia liked to visit us, briefly, most days, to keep us abreast with her forays with the aristocracy, until, inevitably, Loopy was invited to her home for afternoon tea. Her afternoon tea, she told us, would spurn the usual scones and cream for some 'rather nice biscuits and cucumber sandwiches with the crusts cut off' – more upmarket from the doorsteps and thick slices of ham offered by us. This was no less than her friends would expect, she explained tapping her scarlet manicured nails on our kitchen table. The F/H/B was inquisitive, 'What for?' he wanted to know, 'ain't they got no teeth?'

'Of course they've got teeth,' she replied indignantly. 'The Queen always has the crusts cut off her cucumber sandwiches.' Then, as an aside snipe at the F/H/B, she added loftily, 'These people are semi-intellectuals, you know.'

'You mean half-wits?' queried the F/H/B, ramming his cap on his head and making for his boots in the back doorway, his patience at an end. Truth to tell, he empathised with Richard alternating between, 'poor bugger' and 'silly old sod' for being browbeaten by a woman.

Richard was built like a sprout stalk, almost frail and shrunken in his thinness, incredibly polite, and newly retired at sixty-five. He and his wife were like chalk and cheese and I liked them both, enormously. The first time we saw them they were walking down the lane outside our back door, something no stranger ever did without being sighted by the F/H/B. Coming from a town, they seemed unsure whether to speak or not, but the F/H/B soon settled that score, with a direct, 'Who be you?' They explained they had bought the house nearby and introduced themselves at which the F/H/B said, 'Well you'd better come in and have a cuppa tea and tell us your business, 'twill save us a lot of time finding out.' They told us that Richard had travelled for his shipping firm for many years, mainly visiting the USA, Sweden and Australia, all places where some of the business and all of the social side was conducted in fairly convivial circumstances. Patricia had planned her own life in London, being interested in art, flower arranging, garden plants and high fashion. And drinking, we found out later. They told us they had managed to bring some of their garden plants with them, including a rare ivy which had stayed undamaged in transit, and had been left on their patio overnight. The next morning all that was left in the plant pot was the stick that the ivy had climbed around, and standing beside it was a rather untidy sheep satisfactorily chomping its lips, with little bits of their precious ivy trailing from the corners of its mouth. One of ours, without doubt and from the description we recognised Old Granny, a martinet of an old ewe, with one eye and dangling wool from breaking through any hedge that was a challenge, and an appearance like a piece of untidy knitting.

We apologised and they took it very well, saying they realised that these kinds of things might happen in real countryside, but they just were not prepared for a visitation from a hungry sheep so soon. We explained guiltily that Granny was not motivated by hunger and although she only had one eye, that did not impede her. There was nothing wrong with her snifter, and she aimed determinedly for any new delicacy, be it near at hand or up and over a hedge. Patricia told us the only animal they had ever owned was a cat which had died some years previously.

'A tabby alley cat, that's all he was,' she continued in her plummy tones. 'A boy at our son's school gave it to him, although, when one thinks of it, the boy's mother was a countess.' I dare not look at the F/H/B, but I caught Richard's face as he opened his mouth to say something, then thought better of it, which more or less set the pattern for our new neighbours' behaviour in the years to come. It also gave us an insight into the difficulties of uprooting and moving to a new area at retirement age, in their case an area which offered them none of the interests they had acquired in town. In fact, Richard told us he had lived his life, with no interests or hobbies other than his work, which was shipping, and from which he was heartily glad to walk away from when he retired. It was, he went on extremely stressful, alleviated by heavy drinking bouts with those with whom he did business, particularly the Swedes and Australians. We soon noticed that this was the part of his work he still adhered to in his retirement. His wife, alone in London for weeks on end, belonged to clubs and art classes and generally filled what could have been an empty life. Her husband expected her to move to a country cottage – anywhere, he didn't know where – drop her London life, and devote her time to him in an idyllic retirement. The whole exercise, it soon became obvious to us, was going to take more than a dream to succeed; it was uphill all the way and then some. Nevertheless, they were not alone in their turmoil; it is unbelievable the tiny amount of thought some people put into retirement into an area completely unknown to them – some of them might as well be in China. One couple had decided together to drive from home until they made a decision, unanimously, wherever they ran out of petrol. They landed up in Dulverton, visited an estate agent, bought a property, moved in and hated it, wailing that nobody had told them they were next to a holiday cottage and the nearest Woolworth's was twenty-six miles away at Taunton. They stayed all of eighteen months. The Dulverton locals shook their heads over and over again repeating, 'Us see 'em come in over the bridge and us see 'em go out over the bridge.' Those incomers made of sterner stuff grit their teeth and see it through, appreciative of all the countryside has to offer and determined to give it their best shot. Whilst some come to Exmoor for the deer, the sheer beauty of it, and the hunting, others have no idea these things are part of it.

Patricia and Richard also remained our neighbours for many years, although, we suspected, more on a basis of not knowing where else to go, but they were good neighbours and entered into the Exmoor spirit of entertaining with drinks evenings, although us locals were kept strictly separate from mingling with their titled friends. They were generous hosts and I well remember one night when we were invited to visit, together with the delightful elderly sisters who lived at the farm across the road. They were little ladies and they dressed much alike, wearing their best brown bootees in winter for special occasion visits, their black ones for fleeting visits. Every time they visited me, before I as much as greeted them, my eyes would flash to their feet to see which boots they were wearing – long-stay or short-stay. They told us to call them Auntie Julie and Auntie Dolly and it is no exaggeration to say we grew to idolise them. On the particular night we partied at Richard and Patricia's our generous hosts topped up our glasses again and again, Auntie Julie declaring her delight at gin and tonic. She told us afterwards they both found it a little strange to be invited to a party at which there was no food, other than crisps and as our hostess generously put it, 'some rather nice nuts'. Auntie Dolly's and her sister's parties comprised vast bellyfuls of grub, washed down with copious amounts of cider, so they were not unused to alcohol. Perhaps it was just the gin that had the amazing effect on the pair of them, but Auntie Julie in particular, who was sitting next to me and suddenly seemed to be shrinking downwards. Or perhaps it was the brandy I was drinking that caused this apparent phenomenon, until I realised she was not exactly shrinking, but just sliding slowly under the table. Nobody else seemed to miss her and she carefully placed her empty gin glass on the table. When she had disappeared gently and quietly completely under the table I caught the F/H/B's eye and pointed. He said something like, 'Oh my gorsey,' and came round, putting both his hands under her armpits and hauled her out. Auntie Julie was paralytic but happy, with a half-smile on her face. The F/H/B as usual, was well in command of the situation, a quick thinking tough guy at his best in adversity. Home for the sisters was only a stone's throw away and the F/H/B, in charge, ordered me to go down the hill to fetch our wheelbarrow 'and put plenty of hay in, Maid, us don't want Auntie covered in bumps and bruises when her comes to.' Whilst I was passing our back door I did a quick change from my best shoes into my welly boots, then into the yard to collect the wheelbarrow and the hay, then the big push up the road to take on board the cargo.

Auntie Joo was carefully loaded and I held her steady as the F/H/B pushed and we all accompanied the entourage with Auntie Joo's little legs ending in her best brown boots dangling over the side, through the sisters' yard and up the passage they called the drainery, into the back door. Auntie Dolly who could walk, just, was supported by Patricia and Richard, looking by then as if she weren't too sure if it was Christmas or Easter. The F/H/B and I went back to finish our drinks, and then have 'one for the road', by which time the wheelbarrow looked almost inviting. 'Shall I get in?' I asked. 'No, Maid,' he answered, 'us'll leave 'n there till the morning 'cos I'd never pass the breathalyser!'

The next morning we called on the sisters to check their state of health and there was Auntie Joo, chirpy as a cricket – she obviously had no memory of her journey home, only of what a great night they had both had. 'When I die,' she announced, her little bright bird like eyes twinkling, 'I want to die partying!'

Christmas, as I said somewhere else, commences on December 1st and finishes March 1st, just before preparations are beginning for lambing. Exmoor womenfolk are involved in a flurry of preparations for the festival, as it goes without saying every single item of food is home-made, many from recipes handed down from mother to daughter for generations. Farmer carries on with his work as usual, though keeping it down to the barest basics on Christmas Day and Boxing Day – two days of the winter when he's not likely to be seen out hedging. On the whole, farmers are uninterested in Christmas, viewing it as an unnecessary disruption to their work schedule, although the F/H/B always vowed his enjoyment of the holiday period as, like most other farmers, the hard graft of Christmas passes them by: no cards to write (Missus does them all) no presents to buy – (leave it to Missus) no shopping, and the present he is expected to buy for missus, is usually something practical for the farm. My sister-in-law received a load of chippings for the farm drive one year, and next year her husband discovered a pair of free gloves given away with Slaymore Rat Poison, which he handed over to her for a Christmas present. 'Her was delighted,' was his self-satisfied comment. Less delighted was Patricia when Richard handed her a cheque for £100 to buy herself a present. 'He would, wouldn't he,' she sighed heavily. 'What's a hundred pounds? It's neither one thing nor another.' The F/H/B gave me the little electronic egg whisk, which I really coveted, and Aunt Dolly and Aunt Julie gave me a little red tea caddy that I cherish to this day.

Somehow there's always a little of the feeling that once Christmas Day is over and done with we can let go and enjoy ourselves on Boxing Day at the meet in the Square. Christmas Day evening is spent brushing and shampooing horses' manes and tails, and everyone is up and about first thing the next morning. The air of expectancy is such as on no other day, and crowds of people turn out to cheer the Hunt riding into town for the most important day of the year, the masters and huntsman sporting red Father Christmas hats. A collection that day is held for the Hunt staff, and people have always been generous with their gifts. The Lion Hotel provides hot mulled wine, and it is usually some time before the Master thanks them for their generosity and the crowd for turning out, and the Hunt finally moves off, followed by the field, to circle the village, the little moorland town reverberating to the stirring sound of clattering hooves and the huntsman blowing the horn whilst the crowd clap and cheer themselves hoarse.

The next big celebration is New Year, and I well remember us inviting six friends in 1977 to stay for New Year. None of them had a lot of time to spare, but could manage three nights, which would see us out of the old year and into the new one. The first night on 30 December was to be our get-together party night, the second, New Year's Eve we planned to go to the dance in Dulverton, and the third day was set aside for recovery. It was not to be. Nature intervened. On that first evening light snow commenced to fall to cries of 'look how pretty the little flakes are!' I tried not to find the word 'little' disturbing, but it reminded me of an old Chinese proverb, 'Little snow, big snow, big snow little show', which in the past had always proved positive. The smaller the flakes the heavier the fall, and never more so than on this night. The light covering increased steadily to a heavy fall, and by the morning the whole landscape had changed to what looked like a film set of the Swiss Alps. It was frosty and freezing cold and, although we had no central heating in the old farmhouse, this was balanced to a certain extent by our visitors who willingly recruited themselves into a little army carrying logs from the shed across the yard to stoke the fires in the house. Supplies of food and fuel were not a problem as country folk are always prepared in winter for such emergencies.

With yet another fall of snow from a blackening sky our guests reconciled themselves to making the best of their soon to be extended three-night holiday. They stayed for ten. It was during this period that the F/H/B decided we should all have a treat by eating Gossy our one goose, for dinner. We had postponed that pleasure, waiting for a suitable occasion, and this, the F/H/B deemed, was it. We had never attempted to rear geese until Gossy arrived the previous summer in the egg stage, from a farmer friend in Leicester, who suggested a broody bantam could just about sit on the one big egg and then rear the gosling. The egg duly hatched a fine gosling, and the little bantie hen clucked and fussed over her baby, which grew at an incredible rate until he was about six weeks old when he was bigger than his adoptive mother and she took against him, pecking ferociously at the youngster and taking little runs at him to drive him away. We named him Gossy and fed him separately from the hen flock, as they were all ganged up against him and refused to share a morsel of their corn with the fast-growing gander, who, although towering over them was terrified when they attacked him, en masse, led by Mummy.

Returning from market one Saturday we found an odd-shaped bundle moving slightly beside the kitchen Rayburn, wrapped in a towel. Closer inspection revealed a soaking wet Gossy, head flopping and a near-death look. There was a note on the table from our neighbour Seemingly, reading simply and uninformatively 'bird near drowned', which served to fuel our curiosity as to what had happened to the gosling. Seemingly called later and explained that he 'just happened' to be in our yard (at lunchtime) when he heard the squawking of a bird in distress, and the angry cries of hens, and found the disturbance was at the water trough. Gossy had decided on a dip, but in no time the oblong trough had been surrounded by the aggressive banties who refused to let him clamber out, pecking him from all four sides and, Seemingly added, trying to push him under, with some success. Seemingly rescued Gossy, who had probably been in there for some time and was exhausted, and he carried the cold wet bird into the kitchen with the presence of mind of a true countryman and gave him a hot bath in the sink, and then dried him as best he could in our roller towel. The bird recovered, but continued to lead a very unhappy life, a victim of non-stop bullying by little bantie hens. Gossy never stood up to them, and used to look up at me unblinkingly when I urged him, 'Go on, stand up to them, you're bigger than they are, fight dirty if you have to,' but he always backed down.

And on that day in January Gossy's end was decided, with the F/H/B uttering, 'Poor little bugger,' as he slit his throat.

He was plucked and left to settle in the dairy for a couple of days, and he weighed in at 13lbs on the kitchen scales, which was surprising. The full impact of poor Gossy's miserable little existence never really hit me until I was stuffing him with sage and onions, and I felt traitorous. He had looked on me as a friend and I had betrayed his trust. The tears started falling, as they are now as I write this, and that night the F/H/B carved him up but I had lost my appetite for goose...

Nevertheless, with our friends staying everybody made the best of their incarceration, and it was Party Night Every Night at Chilcott.

The supplies, mercifully, were holding out despite the influx of six extra marathon eaters fattening up for England. There were swedes and greenstuffs in the garden with the F/H/B's maygrow principle paying dividends (they may grow or may not grow). And the innards of the two freezers filled with pig, lamb and beef were beginning to look like they were sinking alarmingly, but famine did not hit Chilcott. We milked the Jersey cow, made clotted cream twice a day, and collected eggs from the hens that struggled to keep us supplied throughout the bitter cold. The one department that was slightly worrying was the booze, which had been topped up by the visitors, who brought copious supplies with them, but, there was no escaping it, all the party nights were taking their toll.

One morning ITV from Bristol telephoned, enquiring if they might land by helicopter in our front field to film the surroundings. The

F/H/B told them it was impossible, the snow was too deep, plus there was a haze over everywhere obscuring any viewing. They took this as being not wanted, and tried persuasion.

'If there's anything you need in the way of provisions,' wheedled the spokesman, 'we'll be glad to bring it for you.'

The F/H/B was unhesitating, 'Right, Squire, that'll be a case of whisky and a box of cigars.'

'But what about provisions?' persisted the voice at the Bristol end.

'I just told 'ee,' said the F/H/B in the voice he used to not very bright ten-year-olds. 'A case of whisky and a box of cigars.'

He never did pick up those all-important provisions, because landing was impossible, but when one door closes, as they say, another opens, and two days later the drinks cupboard was right up to capacity, ready to survive anything that hit us for the next month. Fate can intervene in many mysterious ways and this time it appeared in the form of a smooth-haired Jack Russell called Parsnip.

The little bitch was the property of our friend and neighbour, Gill, who lives at the next farm, the entrance to which is protected by a cattle grid. This was not protection enough against our sheep dog, Skipper, who actually fell through the cattle grid, straddling it, striving to get at the little bitch, until his cries were heard and he was eventually rescued and hauled out by his collar and tail. Even this did nothing to dampen his ardour, and he reached his goal and had his wicked way. There was consternation all round, Parsnip's owner telling us she thought Skipper ought to have learnt his lesson after falling down the cattle grid and that he was a dirty old man who ought to have given up on bitches years before, and the F/H/B pointing out that, owing to the difference in their sizes, copulation could only have taken place if Parsnip had given him the come-hither by climbing on to a bag of King Edwards. The outcome was a consultation with our vet over the pregnancy, with a decision by the vet to perform a Caesarean operation on THE DAY. As these things do the little Jack Russell began her labour when we were all snowed in. It was early afternoon, and as the owner of Daddy, I felt I should face up to my responsibilities. Gill and I decided to carry the mother-to-be up to the top road, where it was thought possible to drive a Land Rover down to Dulverton, but first we had to surmount the Swiss Alps, which took about an hour to cover just over half a mile, with Parsnip in a zip-up shopping bag which we carried between us, her little white head hanging over the side. We made it to the vet's, who was ready to carry out the Caesarean, and he told Gill to phone in the evening and to collect the animals the next day. We had never before seen the village under so much snow, great banks of it lining the roads where the snowplough had swept it up. It looked like the last outpost in Alaska. We filled the bag with fresh supplies of what we needed most (whisky) and set off for home. That evening the vet rang to tell Gill that Parsnip had given birth to two sizeable puppies, the breeding anything but pure but never mind, they were sturdy and healthy.

The next day Seemingly announced that at lunchtime he would be taking his tractor to Dulverton and visiting the pub. We all went, leaving home early to climb the Swiss Alps, which were higher than the top of the hedge, joining the tractor on the top road. There was room for everybody; those that couldn't squeeze into the transport box on the back clung to the mudguards, with the luckier ones in the cab. It was a lovely bright day with a cloudless blue sky, but bitterly cold, so we were glad to park the tractor alongside several others, and pile into the warmth of the pub. We told everybody we were on a mission to collect newborn puppies, and rounds of drinks kept coming up 'to wet the babies' heads'.

We all celebrated, but none more so than Gill and myself with something akin to self-satisfaction. We had surmounted the Swiss Alps; the little bitch had survived what we expected to be a difficult birth. We all dispersed eventually, the visitors and Seemingly to restock on liquid supplies, and Gill to collect Parsnip and the pups, eventually regrouping. When Gill returned there was the little dog in the shopping bag, her head hanging out of one end, and Gill wiping away a tear.

'All that,' she said, mournfully, 'and she's eaten them. The vet left them last night and by this morning they had gone.'

There was nothing left to say, just commiserations and brandies all round to set us up with inner warmth for the freezing journey home. We arrived indoors to meet a small but fast-running river coursing across the kitchen flagstones from its source behind the adjoining dairy door. There was a gaping hole in the dairy ceiling and the dairy looked more like a bomb had hit than a flood. Water pipes upstairs had frozen and in the bedroom above the dairy a plug had been left in the washbasin with the frozen tap still left turned on. The afternoon sun had warmed the frozen pipes (we had seven bursts over the period altogether) and the rest, as they say, was history. The bedroom was wrecked, the dairy was wrecked, the kitchen was awash, the old dog had suffered the indignity of the cattle grid to no avail and then had his bed washed away in the flood. There are times when life can seem quite unfair.

Our guests managed to manoeuvre their cars up the icy road after a visit by the snowplough. They were all business people who had to explain daily by phone their incarceration to their disbelieving employers, and eventually how a three-night stay had metamorphosed into a ten-night house party. They hardly looked like they had been enjoying a relaxing holiday, in fact they seemed quite pale and pinched as they took careful little steps down the garden path to clear the snow off their cars in preparation for their homeward journeys. Hungover would have been an exaggeration; they were suffering more from what the F/H/B called a dose of late-night shivers. The two of us were fine, but then we had served our apprenticeship in partying thanks to our tutors, Auntie Dolly and Auntie Julie. We waved our friends goodbye regretfully.

◇◇◆◇◇

January had to be the worst month to make a move, particularly to a damp West Country area, and even more so with a change of occupation, akin, I would say to venturing into a foreign country with a whole new set of rules and de-motion in status. In the 1950s a Government Scheme ground into operation to train ex-servicemen to become farmers. They were assigned to working farms and at the end of that twelve-month training they were expected to emerge fully-fledged farmers capable of running their own business. Two ex-Army majors were assigned to North Devon, one to the F/H/B's family farm, the other nearby at Uncle's farm. They moved, together with their glamorous blonde wives and their immaculate children, out of London (Mayfair) and into two farm cottages at the beginning of January. It was cold and wet; neither cottage had electricity (which they only discovered on arrival when they had to go straight to bed as it was already dark). There were no bathrooms, no hot-water system, and the lavatory was a privy at the end of the garden. The two ex-Army officers started work the next morning at their respective farms, and each was sent out into a muddy farmyard with a shovel scraping mud, possibly the most hideous of farm jobs, the one task any farmer will offload onto any likely-looking biddlehead that happens along. When the yards were eventually cleared, the two apprentices were promoted to a higher standard, learning to milk cows, clean shippons and feed the bullocks. Every night they went home exhausted. With no baths, their wives had to improvise with an old stone-built furnace in a washhouse which they would fill with cold water, then light the fire underneath with chippings and sticks they gathered from a nearby wood and keep stoking until their husbands arrived home, took off all their clothes and climbed naked into their respective furnace, where each straightaway fell asleep. Major Geoff's cottage was semi-detached, and their neighbour was another farm labourer, his wife and large family. Major Geoff's wife, although finding a country life alien to all she had even known was determined to integrate, but did remonstrate with Uncle over the toilet facilities. Their privy was a ramshackle little shed at the bottom of the garden, with a paper-thin wooden partition down the middle, thus dividing it into two. This, she said, she did not mind at all, but she found it acutely embarrassing to often find herself walking down the shared path side-by-side with the father-of-seven from next door.

'There's not even a lock on the door,' she complained to Uncle, who pushed his check cap to the back of his head, looking puzzled.

'There's never been a lock on thik door,' he explained, 'there's nort there to pinch!'

The other lady, Major Reg's wife, was often to be seen walking the road when the wind was up north. The down-draught with smoke and smuts from the solid-fuel cooker (which was all they had for heating) was so unbearable that she used to dress herself and her children in their warmest clothes and go walkabout.

The two ex-Army comrades finished their twelve-month training, bought a farm and set up in partnership together, which, sadly through their inexperience, was a total disaster. Farming cannot be learnt in twelve months, nor, is it likely, in twelve years. They lost their hay to a wet summer and were unlucky with some of their bought-in cattle. Money was so tight that they even milked off a cow that lay dead in its field. The two wives then decided to set up together in their own profession which was hairdressing, and which saved them all from bankruptcy. From a small beginning in their farmhouse sitting room they were so hugely successful that they eventually ran a small chain of hairdressing salons in North Devon, winning nationwide competitions and fame with staff they trained themselves. The two husbands found other jobs, one in accountancy and the other as a car salesman; perhaps they should have started in that direction when they left the Army instead of diverting into the unknown and hazardous. But would you believe it, to this day both the wives declare wholeheartedly that the twelve months of deprivation they spent in their cottages and pre-farming were without doubt the happiest twelve months of their lives. They may have lost all their money trying to farm, but they were survivors and started out over again, this time in their own medium, thankfully a successful one.

The date they moved in – and out – of their farm enterprise would almost certainly have been 25 March, Lady Day. A few moved farms at Michaelmas, but Lady Day was always the prime moving date, not only for changing farms, but for farm workers changing jobs. Years back a good farm labourer would often be poached to work elsewhere, perhaps with the offer of a better cottage, or one with a bigger garden. A horse and cart would be loaned by his new employer and all his furniture loaded and removed to the new abode, plus the family (some with as many as ten children). There were no family allowances then but there were 'perks' – either a free tied cottage, or one with a minimal rent, deducted from wages, free milk and usually a couple of lengthy rows of potatoes from the field crop. The workers always seemed to grow acres of beetroot in their cottage garden, which would often be boiled together with the potatoes in great saucepans, which had the effect of turning the potatoes pink. Back then every event included skittling for a pig, and many a pig was reared in a shed at the end of the garden, so no scraps were ever wasted – more what we now call recycled. The farm workers who were unmarried and lived home with Mum and Dad had wealth beyond the wildest dreams of the farmers' sons, being paid the allotted agricultural wage, whilst farmers' sons were doled out meagre pocket money – no more than £1 per week. They supplemented this by catching rabbits to sell, and some lads like the F/H/B owned a pony, trained up after hours of practice, often in the evenings, to win gymkhana prizes. This was as much business as pleasure, the first prize in the main events being £1 – the equivalent of a whole week's wages! The money prizes at pony events today are virtually the same, the one area where the pound has actually risen in the face of inflation. Money is not so important now that there is more of it about; most sporting competitors are chasing the coveted rosette and even the 'teenies' on their expensive ponies at gymkhanas get a rocket from Mummy if they don't try hard enough.

In the circumstances, it is not surprising that farmers used to be very careful indeed over money, forever instilling into their wives the need for frugality. The one area years ago that was worth concentrating on was inheritance; it was important to 'leave' money, and if you stood a chance of being the richest man in the churchyard, then bully for you. Folk counted on inheriting from maiden aunts, grannies, anybody who was thought to constantly save, even if it meant they lived all their lives if not in poverty then in frugal economy. It was then expected for the beneficiary not only to keep that money, but also to add to it before passing it on down the line.

Sundays would often be set aside to visit the maiden aunts, the children (the F/H/B was one, along with his brother and sister) dressed in their best Sunday clothes, sitting stiffly on wooden upright chairs in freezing front parlours that smelt of mothballs, and kept strictly for the Sunday visitors, Mother and Father attempting some stilted conversation with Auntie thus ensuring she never changed her will. Sometimes tea would be made and cake handed round, and once, the F/H/B remembered, a glorious fruit-filled Christmas cake that took centre place on the table and he, as his Mother reminded him afterwards, brought shame on the family by asking for a slice. He was refused, as Auntie said the cake was not to be eaten that day, so nobody got any and all everybody got was just another Arrowroot biscuit. They did get the money, though, after enduring years of Sunday visits, eventually, when Auntie died at ninety-five. The money made not the slightest difference to the F/H/B and his brother and sister, as Mother saved it, which was a foregone conclusion. It was certainly never squandered on expensive presents for the children, or any presents at all for that matter.

The money benefited them indirectly as farmers' sons were always set up in farming when they married, the older son taking over the family farm and the younger one being bought a farm in the same area, on which he paid interest to Father. Daughters did not get jobs outside farming, they stayed home and helped Mother, which meant getting all the meals for the menfolk as they were always termed, the 'menfolk' consisting of the immediate family plus all the casual labourers who were frequently employed. There would often be a 'boy-chap' also living in the house that fetched and carried wood for the fires and generally attended to odd jobs. 'Casual labour' included thresher men who would turn up for two days at a time and stay overnight, wanting their breakfast at seven in the morning before they started up their vast threshing machines to commence the day's work. All the neighbours would be booked to help once the thresher swung into action, so they also had to make an early start as it would be winter and they would have their cows to milk and stock to feed before they left home. They would be allocated their jobs on arrival, pitching sheaves to the thresher, or two of them on the top of the machine cutting the binds on the sheaves – oats or barley usually in this area – or, the worst job for late arrivals, at the back on the chaff, or heaving the filled bags as it threshed.

Then there were the rats to be dealt with that had nested all winter in the rick, and those folk that didn't wear gaiters had to remember to tie their trouser legs tightly round their boots as fleeing rats tended to disappear up them as a refuge. Major Reg was said to be horrified to see one local thresher man pick up a rat in his hand and kill it by biting its neck. Major Reg also told of his first days threshing as being a revelation into hard work, the dust, the din and the rats. He marvelled at the food that was put away, with a stop for 'forenoon' at eleven o'clock, yeast buns, sandwiches and cakes and tea, then a full-blown roast dinner for 12 or 14 workers at one o'clock, where they all got round the vast kitchen table and were waited on by the women-folk.

He was reported to have said afterwards, 'My dear old boy, I might have been in China, I couldn't understand a word they said.' At the end of the day a vast tea was laid out in the farmhouse before the neighbours and threshers departed back to their own farms. The invention of the combine harvester changed the whole face of thresh-ing, particularly for the womenfolk, with the numbers to feed greatly reduced and all the horrors of threshing day eliminated forever. The farmers' daughters who 'helped out' at home usually couldn't wait to get away, and only marriage pointed the way to salvation. But it was invariably to a farmer's son, and the whole grinding routine swung back into action as soon as they set up in their own farm.

Young people's get-togethers were no more a problem years ago than they are now, except that then they cycled to their Young Farmers' Club meetings and dances whereas now they pile into old bangers or Father's Land Rover. Then, as now, there was always market-day when conversations are easily struck up between the young men and women with such stimulating/provocative openers as 'what sort of worm drench do you use?' As winter wears on, so do the functions, some tending to veer towards a more commercial slant, though these are mainly for the ladies entertaining their friends at Tupperware parties (who, I think triggered off the home party system) make-up, fashion jewellery and even, unbelievably, sex aids (the lady who promoted the latter was an incomer with a shorter-than-usual shelf life after THAT party). If sex-aids do not figure high, neither does jewellery on a country lady's list of priorities. At one party we all tried various necklaces and bracelets on (should ankle chains be worn inside or outside welly boots?). One large farm girl looked quite stunning in a pair of clip-on earrings that we all tried to persuade her to purchase. She was resolute that she had never worn such appendages in her life, but capitulated under pressure with 'OK, in my ears one day, up a pig's ass the next.'

She pronounced 'ears' as 'years', which added to the hilarity. We wondered if her prophecy proved true as none of us ever saw those earrings again.

Valentine's Day on 14 February might be considered by some to be a great date for a party, but on the countryman's calendar it slips past virtually unnoticed. That's because he might be expected to resuscitate romance by buying a card and even penning a message to Missus, but just mention the word romance and back comes, 'There's nort in this old love lark, Maid, 'tis all down to h'economics.' Just so long as the h'economics stretch to a special home-made cake to mark the occasion at teatime, which incidentally, he tackles with gusto, pandering to his sweet tooth and always remembering a good cake should be like silage, with the juice running out. This usually signifies the end to a non-event. When we were first married I used to give the F/H/B a card, all hearts and flowers, but I gave up when he said he had never sent a Valentine card in his life and had no intention of starting, particularly after marriage.

The phrase he used which killed it stone dead was, 'You don't give a fish a worm after you've caught'n.'

Years after, though, somebody actually sent him a card which caused plenty of speculation, particularly as the postmark was indecipherable.

The card appeared innocuous enough, bearing on the outside the printed message 'you are more than just a dream'. Then inside in big red letters 'you're a nightmare' and two Xs. He loved it and treasured it for weeks, showing to everybody that came in. The national newspapers have managed over the years to turn Valentine's Day into a special, i.e. commercial festivity. Advertisements offer two nights in Paris (the subtlety not lost on those that are eager Valentines, the operative word being 'nights' when the rest of the year two days in Paris is the usual wording). When I broached the advertisement the F/H/B said what would us do in thik old place filled with foreigners you got to shout at to get 'em to understand. So how about a week on the Nile? 'Hev you gone stark raving bonkers?' he wanted to know… Was I or was I not the one who was sick on Ilfracombe pier, just looking out over at the heaving sea so for God's sake woman, forget any seafaring nonsense. In fact, forget any nonsense at all and stay home to work.

I well remember one dull Monday morning on 14 February when the F/H/B announced he was off to the village, as it was a non-hunting day, and was there anything I needed? Yes, I told him, I would appreciate a bunch of flowers collected from our lady florist-cum-greengrocer, aware that he regarded buying flowers as sissy, so they would go onto my monthly account. When he eventually arrived back home my eyes must have bulged like chapel hat pegs when he squeezed sideways through the kitchen door carrying in both hands a truly magnificent bouquet of colourful flowers, comprising mimosa, narcissi, pink tulips and daffodils. I shoved aside the pudding I was mixing, wiped my hands on my British Beef plastic pinny, and flung my arms round his neck. At last, I thought wildly, I'm a Valentine, loved, cherished and above all, desired. 'Wonderful, wonderful,' were the only words I could get out, and was slightly surprised that my hero did not seem exactly bowled over by my unusually warm reception in the middle of the morning.

'Half a minute, Maid,' he said, "t'in quite what you'm thinking,' and as he laid the flowers carefully on the kitchen table I could see that it was not, in fact, a bouquet at all, but a wreath with a black-edged Deepest Sympathy card attached to a delicate fern.

'You see, Maid,' he went on, 'there was this wreath left over from a funeral on Saturday and Pauline thought you'd just as soon have'n as a bunch of flowers. And 'tis free!'

There we go again, I thought, deflated, there's that word farmer's favour more than any other. Nevertheless, I was delighted with my lovely flowers and picked them all carefully from the wreath to arrange in vases. The sequel came a week later after we had gone to bed. I was relaxing reading the daily newspaper with the F/H/B snoring peacefully beside me, when I caught a headline that made me shoot bolt upright. It read, 'Husband gives wife wreath then shoots her'. I glanced down at my sleeping farmer and thought no, never, he couldn't be bothered.

One farmer's wife did tell how she seized the initiative to resuscitate honeymoon magic by booking herself and her F/H/B into a hotel for the weekend, to include a Saturday night dance. The music strummed romantically, couples whirled and twirled, the wife sipped a Babycham and her partner downed a couple of pints of his usual super-phosphate to get in dancing mode. Then reluctantly, he took to the floor with as much enthusiasm as a trailer load of King Edwards – meanwhile, upstairs staff were turning back their bed with the husband's pyjamas artfully arranged and displaying a thrifty patch with an old flour bag printed THIS WAY UP.

Now that line-dancing has hit Exmoor the menfolk seem relieved that their women can enjoy dancing without them which is a definite plus, but there's always a minus, in this case being that the womenfolk's thoughts are turning to whole weekends away, some abroad. Even the F/H/B reckons you give a woman an inch and they take 10 yards, and you want to keep clear of that old foreign lot, "Tis all rum, bum and gramophone records, and the next day all you've got is a thick head and rumbling guts because none of 'em eat proper food, 'tis just cauch with a spoonful of rice they don't even put jam on. Why can't they just stop home and look after their man? What's WRONG with today's women?'

Spring (1)
Horseplay and Harmonies

With spring in the air Exmoor braces itself for a season of horseplay, the horse being as much a part of the moor as the wild red deer. Point-to-points get off to an early start, followed by gymkhanas and horse shows and, usually at the end of the summer season, sponsored rides, with enthusiasm for one and all at fever pitch. They all agree 'tis easier to find a second-hand woman than a second-hand horse. A certain amount of horse-dealing inevitably precedes these events, which in itself is a tricky test of endurance involving late-night deals and a fair capacity for Famous Grouse. In an area where 'my word is my bond', a handshake is enough to clinch any deal, with the horse changing hands and money following, eventually, when the buyer can manage to raise it. Between the handshake and the cash handover the subject is unmentionable, even if it takes six months (sometimes even longer). The F/H/B had no memory of learning to ride but there is an album with a sepia-tinted photograph of him, little more than a baby with a head of white curls, being held on a tiny Shetland pony by his father who was determined his second son should follow in his footsteps and become a horseman (George, the elder brother by some seven years was more interested in tractors and motor bikes and all things mechanical). Father was not to be disappointed as the young Arthur grew up devoted to horses and competitive riding, hacking miles to gymkhanas at the weekend and spending as many evenings a week practising as the work on his parents' farm allowed. Possibly he had to practise more than most, particularly with flying jumps in and out of the saddle, as he had a displaced hip from birth. It was thought in later life that his father's insistence on placing him astride a pony at such an early age, could have exacerbated his condition, but the F/H/B was eternally grateful to Father for instilling in him his enduring love of horses. Together they did a bit of wheeling and dealing with the boy Arthur, as he became older, graduating to bigger and better animals; a horseman following in his father's footsteps.

They both agreed that one of the most controversial statements ever uttered must surely be 'without doubt that is the finest horse I have ever seen', on a par with 'We are sending a man from the Ministry to help you'. Owning the 'finest horse' doubtless inspires those with decent, ordinary hunters to dream of point-to-points and winning the Members' Race in a blaze of glory. Owners always insist, it's 'just a bit of fun' but the frantic preparations parallel a Grand National marathon with horse and rider inseparable until the great day, when the glory can be fleeting: the rider parading in the paddock at two o'clock, jumping six fences and in hospital by twenty to three, whilst maintaining his horse was not to blame – 'I was just a bit unbalanced.'

As losing is never the fault of the horse, measures are often taken to ensure it gets all the encouragement it needs. One owner with a slow starter was supremely confident that his horse could win if it had a little added impetus at the start. He devised a plan, which entailed training his Jack Russell to jump at the horse's tail in the line-up, which the horse learned to hate and was guaranteed to send it off with a flying start. On the premise that ignorance is bliss; the retained jockey was not informed of this master plan, and on the day of the race lined up confidently at the start, happily unaware that a few yards away a Jack Russell was also under starter's orders, with a scarcely audible 'get him, boy!' The dog launched himself at the horse's tail and the effect was instantaneous, with the horse taking such an almighty leap forward it unseated the jockey, then ran on, riderless, to complete the course. The jockey lay dazed on the ground with the owner, not pleased, bending over him snarling, 'You biddle-head! My horse would have won if you hadn't falled off!'

The same attitude exists in the show ring, where human error shoulders the blame over equine failings.

One country gentleman, watching his wife as she showed her hand-some chestnut, was disappointed to see the horse placed runner up to what he considered to be a plainly inferior winner. But it was the wife who took the full blast of his disappointment. 'You would have won,' he rounded on her afterwards, 'if only you'd been twenty years younger and two stone lighter. Think about it!' But, like the F/H/B and his dad always said, ''tis only a bit of fun'. And never, ever the horse's fault when things don't quite pan out.

Once February fill-dyke is over and done with farmers always hope for a few dry days in March to dry up the ground for their spring sowing. Once the corn is sown everything else seems to fall into place, and in this respect modern machinery can make all the difference, especially if the weather tends to be catchy. Howsoever, some folk never move on from their old entrenched ways, and two of our neighbours across the valley decried all things modern in favour of their old tractor and corn drill, with Missus clinging on the back with one hand and slapping the drill in and out of gear with the other. It was a busy little job because it also entailed keeping an eye on the ten or so outlets as one or more would often jam up. If this was overlooked, time would be the giveaway, indicating all the blank drills when the corn eventually sprouted, and Missus would get a rocket. Our neighbours who favoured the old fashioned drill did, in fact, seem to favour all things bygone. They were a couple who, although 'of an age' married late in life and were so besotted with one another that they both sang love songs all day, with scarcely a pause for breath between each rendition. The music floated our way when the wind was in our direction, and although I would never have described either as a concert singer, I thought it incredibly beautiful that they should even attempt to sing to one another.

The F/H/B was sceptical. 'Lot of bleddy nonsense,' he said, "twill all end in tears, you mark my words.' Even as he spoke we could hear the faint strains of a duet borne on the breeze. It sounded like 'Your tiny hand is frozen', with the wife tra-la-ing. 'Sounds like a sow caught under a gate,' grumbled my unromantic man.

The day they selected to sow their corn dawned bright and breezy, but rain was forecast for the afternoon. Even by the time they started dark clouds were gathering and we could hear their tractor and drill rattling round the field at top speed; it was obviously going to be a race against the rain. I guessed they must have been singing their hearts out, because after a couple of hours I heard the wife let out what I took to be a personal-best high note, followed by great wracking sobs which we had all heard in the past and tended to ignore, accepting that with those two everything was black or white – there was no grey area. The tractor and drill carried on rattling round the field, even as the first splodge of rain fell, but there was no more singing. 'Reckon he've heaved her off round the corner,' cackled the F/H/B, 'listen out for "Goodbye Tootsie bye-bye"!' That night I called to check that all was well and the wife confirmed the F/H/B's prediction that she had been hurled off the corn drill at high speed. Rolling down over the steep field in a heap she had escaped with bruises and spraining her ankle and had to crawl up to the house on her hands and knees, whilst the singing farmer drove straight past her without stopping. Afterwards he said, 'I could see you was all right!'

'As long as I could crawl,' she told me indignantly, 'then I was all right!' She was hurt, she was bitter. The singing stopped for several days, then a small breeze carried on it a waft of a few baritone Tra-la-las. 'Hark to that, Maid,' said the F/H/B, his hand to his ear.

'I can't make it out,' I said, straining to catch the overture selected after the long silence.

'Tee-hee,' laughed the F/H/B. 'By Christ, 'tis what thik old froggie fellow sings – you know, Maid. Cor he ain't half sailing near the wind with that one, I couldn'a picked a blinder like that myself...'

I got it. 'Raindrops keep falling on my head,' I said.

We both collapsed laughing. It was several days after that before a high-pitched screech indicated the baritone was at last joined by his soprano.

Listening to our singing neighbours brought back memories of a couple of holidaymakers who had stayed with us some time before. They were Northcountry, forty-ish, the husband, Mickey, being a small inoffensive man whose hobby was steam engines, whilst his wife, Joanie, was a vast lady who literally swept him out of her path, barging across a room, or even a field, like a battleship on full steam ahead. 'Battleaxe' was the word the F/H/B used.

Everybody knew when she was about to sweep by because she never, ever, stopped humming; not a low, soothing hum but a high pitched, insidious, tuneless hum that penetrated every corner of the house, from the time she got up in the morning until she went to bed at night. Her little husband called her Boss to her face and the Battleaxe behind her back. She drove their car and decided where they should go on their daily trips, without, as far as any of us could see, even consulting Mickey. A musical day shut in the car with Joanie tunelessly humming must have been torture for the game little man. 'And that's not all,' he confided to the F/H/B. 'There's the sex. The minute she gets in bed and stops humming, it's sex. Six bloody years of it I've had, and that's a fact.'

'Chuck her out,' advised the F/H/B.

Mickey shook his head. 'It's all right for you to talk, you don't know what she's like, she'd kill me.'

The conversation ended abruptly as a sonorous humming manifested itself, growing ever louder as Joanie appeared, massive in flowing floral chiffon, and grabbed her little man by his arm. 'Here,' she said, stopping humming for a second, 'I want you. No, not that way, this way.' They started to walk off, Joanie very much in charge. It was too much for the F/H/B and he made his protest. 'Half a minute, Missus,' he said, 'he was just talking to me.'

'Tough,' said Joanie. 'That can wait, I can't. In view of the conversation with Mickey, the F/H/B was left wondering at the urgency of this mission, but it turned out Mickey was dragged off to put on a tie, having had the temerity to appear in public without one.

Salvation manifested itself in the unlikely guise of the Edinburgh Festival, which Joanie attended alone every year. Although she dragged her small husband everywhere else it appeared that the Festival was sacrosanct and he was forbidden to even mention it. Friends hinted darkly at Joanie's motives for attending, and their sentiments were not unfounded when she disappeared virtually overnight to darkest Africa with a drummer she had met at the Festival. Our minds boggled at the picture of Joanie in her flowing chiffon roaming the jungle humming along to the tom-toms. The F/H/B's reaction was typical of his compassion for his fellowmen. 'Poor buggers,' he said, shaking his head sadly, 'poor buggers.' Mickey was unaccountably reported to be heartbroken. We never did find out what became of them.

◇◇◆◇◇

Spring (2)
Seemingly's Fancy

The F/H/B reckons never to invest in anything that eats or wants painting, which is a bit of nonsense in a place like Exmoor where the main investment is in sheep who chomp their way through acres of greenery, whilst the rams' chests are painted annually with a colourful substance known as raddle. That very word has a bawdy ring to it, conjuring up visions of cartoon-like ewes (or yaws, as we call them) at tupping-time frisking their psychedelic behinds in the air, and delightedly bleating, 'I bin raddled!' The EEC, naturally, recommends a change of practice involving pen and paper and complicated lambing forms, scrapping the farmers' hitherto simple formula of the yaws with the red backsides lambing the last week in March and the ones with the blue backsides the first week in April.

As Exmoor men tend to live with their sheep, it is hardly surprising that they smell fresh from the sheep dip, which can have a fairly steadying effect on us womenfolk. Howsoever, in Seemingly's opinion there is a woman for every sheep in the field, a sentiment with which the F/H/B firmly agrees. There's the ample sex-bomb who looks like a million dollars but never quite delivers the goods, producing one pathetic little squit-bang of a lamb each year that looks like it's crossed with a Pekinese. Then there's the sweetly shy one who never wants her undercarriage fiddled with, the bossy one who stands her ground like a militant Labour politician, and the athlete, a long-legged sporting type who sprints an assault course round the lambing shed like there's a bucket of ewe (yaw) mix as first prize for the fastest sheep in the West. And, inevitably, there's the glamorous Granny, sporting the obligatory fringe and dingly-danglies, who gulps down her Lonesome Trail mix and takes to the hills, disappearing without trace until dipping time, tailed by a Little Mistake that looks like Daddy was a bit of rough Granny picked up on her travels. We always seem to have a Granny lurking in the background somewhere, though not exactly merging inconspicuously into it. There never was anything inconspicuous about a Granny sheep, once she gets in the swing of things, and there never will be. You give her an inch and she unravels ten yards of fleece.

I remember one with a pathetic undersized little lamb, bleating hungrily, his sparse little frame not so much covered as smothered in his little woolly jacket hanging down in so many folds that it looked like a hand-me-down from a big-fatso brother. He cut a sad little figure, 'standing on a sixpence', we said, with all four feet touching and his mum spacing herself as far as possible from him. It seemed she was counting on starving him out, because although she had milk a-plenty there was no way she wanted her small child to get at it, galloping off at great speed every time he neared her. The only way to handle the awkward old sheep was to tie baler cord round her neck and let it extend for about ten feet, then four times a day I would grasp Little Miracle, as I called him, under one arm and the three of us would race round the paddock until I was close enough to take aim and jump onto Granny's trailing baler cord and we would both jerk to a halt. In theory, that is. Sometimes the run was short, other times it was prolonged, and once I had gathered up the baler cord Granny would be like a bucking bronco that I had to climb aboard in order to clamp her head firmly between my knees, at the same time shoving the lamb underneath the old sheep to suck with all his might before she telescoped her titties up out of his reach. As she did this I would endeavour to hop off her back before she took off again, but more often than not it was bump-bumpity-bump for the two of us as Granny took off at a gallop, culminating in me being upended on the grass.

Once, Richard, the new-ish neighbour walked into the little field and gawked open-mouthed at me setting off on the merry chase after Granny's length of string. The old sheep was growing smarter by the day and had worked out a new formula of slant-weaving to escape being pulled up and having to supply life-saving milk to her Little Miracle. Ever the gentleman, Richard sturdily placed himself between me and Granny, ordering, 'My dear, go and sit down and leave this to me.' He had obviously been attending to the household tasks Patricia allotted to him and was still wearing his blue-and-white stripy butcher's pinny, a garment of derision to the F/H/B whose jeering remarks ranged from 'petticoat government' to 'make mine a pound of mince, Squire'. As he careered off after the old sheep he showed a burst of speed that surprised me. I think it surprised him too, because he was on that piece of string in double-quick time which somehow wrapped itself tightly round one of his polished welly boots, carting our neighbour bump-bumpity-bump across the small, uneven field like a stripy sprout stalk caught in the wind. His pork pie Harris Tweed hat slipped sideways and disappeared in a muddy morass before Granny finally halted, leaving her hapless burden in a bunch of stringing nettles, calling for help. The plummy voice of Patricia drifted over the hedge as she peered across at the conflict, a Thelwell cartoon come to life, the hungry lamb bleating loudly, the old sheep cropping grass but keeping a wary eye on the rest of us, and our gladiator, somewhat dazed after the inglorious contest, still tightly tethered to his opponent. Patricia sashayed in through the gate, tall and superb as ever in swirling skirts and a big hat, taking in the situation, cool as the proverbial cucumber.

'Norma, dear,' she was saying, 'you don't have to lasso him, I'll give him to you!'

If Richard heard, he gave no indication. I held Granny tight on what was left of her cord, at the same time pushing Little Miracle under to suck his mother, and Patricia stooped to struggle with the string round her husband's boot. 'Oh, Richard,' she remonstrated with him, 'what would the directors of your company think if they had seen this?' It was the only time I even heard him answer her back.

'Well, they're bloody well not likely to are they, so that's a bloody silly hypo-hypo... question.'

'Hypothetical,' she interjected.

'That's what I said,' he answered, sitting up and pulling at the string still attaching him to the sheep. Help was at hand but delayed as the F/H/B arrived, and collapsed laughing for several minutes. I managed to hiss in his ear, 'The poor old chap's all in, so for God's sake don't mention mince.' He dragged off the boot, string and all, and pulled Richard up to his feet by his butcher's pinny. Then he looked him square in the eye, saying, 'Make it a leg of lamb for the weekend,' before collapsing to roll laughing again on the grass. Richard regained his composure, turned to me with as much dignity as he could muster, and said, 'I'm sorry this hasn't worked out as well as we had hoped, my dear, but better luck next time, eh?' As he tottered off the F/H/B shouted after him, 'And you can put a bit of kidney in with it!'

Sheep are now, incredibly, becoming a fashionable accessory, no longer confined to Easter cards and calendars. They climb handles of little pottery jugs, peer from plastic pinnies, and meander in glorious colour across ladies' knitted bosoms. They look cuddly, pristine even, because you cannot smell them, and no layman could ever believe that from day one they are planning their own funeral. Preferably a dramatic one. A seizure at shearing time sends everybody into a panic, or maybe a nice comfy snooze in the sun, on their back. That fools farmer nine times out of ten. On the tenth time the wind stops and it's, 'Tee-hee, that'll cut your profit, boss.' Drowning in the farm spring is as popular as it is spectacular, with the added bonus of giving the kitchen tap water a funny taste.

Whichever way of departing this life is selected, it finishes with a trip in the crowded knacker-wagon to the kennels, and if the back door flies open en route and a couple of bodies roll out and stop the traffic, so what!

Like Seemingly always says, anybody who makes a living off sheep could teach they chaps up Westminster how to run the country. Profitably.

Incomers with no knowledge of farming often appear convinced that sheep are the easy option. They purchase as many ewes as their funds allow, then find out how wrong they are, particularly if they forget, or in some cases do not realise, rams are a necessity. As one farmer said to his new neighbours who had no money left for a ram, 'Goin' to do it yourself then?' Another hiccup can arise at dipping time, more than one newcomer finding a swimming pool one of life's little essentials, but giving no thought to a sheep-dip. One said, 'Well what was wrong with dipping them in the swimming pool?' which he ultimately did, but at monumental cost, the dip itself being phenomenally expensive whilst the greater the expanse of water, the more dip is necessary.

Some farms are close enough together to share dips, and, in fact, several neighbours used our dip at Chilcott. One was a lady farmer who lived a fair distance away, but managed her sheep with the help of her small, rather frightened husband. Each year she arrived in the same sheep-dipping uniform of naily boots, a long thick winter overcoat and a matching brown felt hat. Although it would be July we never saw underneath the overcoat as she never removed it, so we could only assume it must be similar to her outerwear. She fairly bristled aggression, accepting all help as her right, and with a sharp tongue that petrified all comers within its firing range. She would ring the F/H/B as she was leaving her farm so that he could be at the road junction to help her across with the sheep. He was always waiting there on time, except on one occasion when he arrived late to find that Nellie had already navigated the crossroads with the help of her little nervous husband.

The F/H/B was given a dressing-down, the like of which he had never received in his life. 'Fat lot of good you be,' snarled Nellie. "Tin a bit of use you sitting home on your lazy ass when I'm up the road waiting for a silly bugger who never turns up, right now I'm going to have to sit down for a minute and you can start on the sod-assing sheep without me and if there's any missing at the finish, I'll know who's pinched 'em!' All this came out in one long unpunctuated burst and Nellie sat firmly down on the edge of the water trough and pulled her brown felt hat forwards over her eyes to signify the subject was closed.

The F/H/B, whose reputation rested on always having the last word, could not let Nellie's tirade pass without defence. 'Now look here, my dear,' he commenced, addressing the dented crown of the felt hat, 'I was on me way up the road and you forestalled me...'

'Yah,' Nellie interrupted, addressing a pile of sheep droppings on the ground. 'That's 'cos I can move sheep faster than your fat belly can march up the road. Now shut your gurt mouth, I want five minutes' quiet.'

The F/H/B did as he was told.

I pondered for a second if I copied her style whether I might achieve the same success. Upon reflection, I thought not.

The yard was hardly the cleanest place to be at dipping time with sheep queuing across it awaiting their turn, and then being released back to shake off their drips in the outgoing area. A clean invisible disinfectant cloud hovered there for days, both outside and in, permeating every corner of the farmhouse and all the outbuildings. Visitors were warned to watch their step, as it was all too easy to skid on a pile of sheep droppings, albeit deodorised ones.

I always tried to listen out for expected guests arriving so as to be in the yard to warn them of the hazards. One couple who were well versed in navigating sheep's droppings invited us to their wedding, but as usual they lived far away and we could never leave the farm at such a busy time of year. We sent them a card featuring two romantic looking sheep on the outside, and inside our message read, 'May your bridal path be strewn with heaps of good luck!' They knew exactly what we meant.

Another visitor arriving on a dipping day was an Australian. His aunt and uncle, who lived in Sussex, were booked at Chilcott for a week's holiday, a charming elderly couple that we knew well from previous visits. On this occasion they had phoned two days before their holiday to ask if they could bring their nephew from Australia, who had turned up, unannounced, to stay with them. He worked in the outback, they told me, and would love to visit Exmoor with them. They could only hope I had a spare room at such short notice – I did luckily, and the F/H/B and I looked forward to meeting a big tough Aussie from the outback.

On the Saturday the little car with Auntie and Uncle and their nephew pulled into the yard in late afternoon and I ran out to greet them. They were a bright, cheery little couple and I always enjoyed their company, but on this particular visit my attention was riveted on something that unfolded itself from the back seat of the car. Was this vision straight off a film set, or, maybe a male model for Mr Universe, no, more likely a life-guard straight off Bondi beach with that swept-back hair bleached blond in the Australian sun. The square-jawed handsome face was tanned, with brilliant blue eyes the colour of the Southern Ocean, the wide smile revealing perfect white teeth. All this was set off with a hand-trimmed black shirt and trousers to match, and a thick gold chain bearing a medallion round this neck. Auntie proudly introduced her nephew, 'We always call him Bonzo, so you must, too.' I was faintly disappointed at a rather limp handshake, having braced myself for a knuckle-cruncher. The biggest surprise came as we all walked up the yard towards the farmhouse and Bonzo turned to his elderly relatives and squeaked in a falsetto voice, 'Golly, Auntie, I've trodden in a stinky-poo!'

I looked over my shoulder for any sign of the F/H/B, but luckily he was not on hand to hear our latest guest's maiden speech when he arrived at Chilcott.

That evening I fervently hoped Bonzo would stay silent at the dinner table and just sit there looking beautiful. But the F/H/B was nothing if not perceptive and something must have happened that triggered him off as he came from the dining-room in to the kitchen, shaking his head disbelievingly over the pile of plates he was carrying. 'Maid,' he said, 'who the hell hev us got stopping here this week?'

It was no good pretending not to know what he was talking about; evasion never sits easily on a countryman's shoulders.

'He's very pleasant,' I ventured, nervously, awaiting an onslaught. I was not disappointed.

'Yeah, and so's a pot-bellied pig, but that's some use and I can't see a lot of use fer 'ee mimpsing round these parts with oh-look-at-me, Auntie.'

I could only hope for a peaceful week. The next morning some disillusionment followed when I took in Bonzo's early morning tea and caught sight of his magnificent teeth in a little plastic container on his bedside table. Teeth aside, as the week unfolded the Australian proved he was not only a very kindly man but the sort every landlady yearns for. He was a handyman, a first-class handyman, who willingly volunteered his services in that direction.

'Well, he ain't going to volunteer 'em in any other direction, is he,' jeered the F/H/B. 'I'd fire a shot up 'ees backside if I thought he wouldn't enjoy it.'

It was obvious that the F/H/B was jeeringly deriding my new handyman as 'a gurt blouse chap pandering to womenfolk, that's all 'tis, and you'm mazed enough to be took in by 'n.' It certainly suited me to be 'took in' as my man described it, with Bonzo rapidly and expertly knocking up a couple of kitchen shelves that I had begged (he used the word nagged) the F/H/B for during the past ten years, and then cheerfully going on to repair the seat of a chair that had trapped many an unwary person as they slowly sank through to floor level.

I could hardly let the jibes pass without defence. 'Listen,' I snapped, 'now that you've kindly informed me our overseas guest is more She than He why don't you just quit griping and let him get on doing what you can't be bothered with? And while you're about it,' I said, warming up nicely, 'put a smile on your face for a change, just like he do!'

'I'll save it for when the lot collapses,' countered the F/H/B.

The smiles never materialised as everything is still in place to this

very day, and I never divulged the ammunition he would have rel-
ished over the handsome Aussie's teeth in the bedside container. His
secret was safe with me until now.

I just wished I could have had Bonzo around to give me a hand at
spring cleaning time. The F/H/B, like most other farmers, could
break a colt, train a sheepdog and handle a chain-saw, but any suggestion of painting and decorating or a bit of carpentry would be
enough to send him off at the double in a cloud of dust and small
stones. The togetherness that binds country husbands and wives
takes a severe knocking even when Missus decides to go it alone and
confine herself indoors to attend to the springtime clean-out.
According to the menfolk's country code of conduct, if you're shut up
inside then you can't be doing a lot, and if you got nothing to do your
man is guaranteed to find you a job outside. Sometimes 'tis just to
stand there in the yard, with features sorrowfully arranged, to give
him somebody to swear at, or, as with the F/H/B something more
positive, like a bit of creosoting.

'Git yer brush and creosote, Maid, and come down and give me a
hand,' he'll say, then I'm no sooner brushing and painting than he
takes off and disappears across the fields, and that's the last I see of
him before dinner. Howsoever, there was one memorable occasion,
some time in the 1980s when I recall slapping away at my creosoting
on the old pigs' house with the temperature soaring to an all-time
high. It was sultry, it was peaceful, the only other signs of life being a
few hens scratching out dust baths, and a couple of cats stretched out
in the shade, so, on a mad impulse, I took it into my head to run
upstairs and slip on my old bathing suit which I found rolled up in the
back of the wardrobe. It filled me with a glorious sense of freedom to
step out of my workaday corduroys and hot sticky pullover into the
sleeveless, legless, ventilated – there was a scattering of moth-holes –
little number that in an instant elevated me from the mundane to the
daring. I flitted out of the bedroom feeling like a mettlesome filly,
charging down the stairs and into my welly boots before crossing the
yard back to my bucket and brush in the pigs' house. Feeling light-
hearted and lightweight I slapped on creosote with a happy new
vigour. That is until I heard the chug-chug of a tractor pulling up
outside the yard gate, and, knowing I hardly looked like Miss World
1985, or even Miss World 1925, I slipped inside the pigs' house. In the

distance, getting ever nearer, I could hear a man's voice calling 'Yoo-hoo, yoo-hoo.' 'Yoo-hoo to you too,' I thought, pressing myself flat against the wall and waiting for him to disappear. I peeped round the door, curious to see who was calling, and spotted Seemingly, standing with his back to me, cap in one hand, scratching his head with the other. Seemingly, I knew, would be unlikely to leave until after dinner, so I looked round, embarrassed, for a cover-up. All I could see was an old mackintosh hanging on a nail that looked of the same era as my bathing suit, stiff and mummified with age, a likely shelter over the years for homeless rodents, roosting bats and itinerant emmets.

In view of the overwhelming odds, there could only be one decision, and I took it. I made a run for the back door at about the same time as Seemingly decided to try the front door. As I opened the back door into the kitchen he opened the front door into the kitchen and our eyes met across the draining board. Neither of us said a single word. It seemed an eternity before my legs motivated into carrying me across the kitchen and up the back stairs to the safety of my corduroys and indestructible socks. To his credit Seemingly never mentioned my embarrassment to the F/H/B, and neither did I. The feeling was probably mutual that he would have been less than approving of my little jolly around the yard in a bathing suit. In my mind I blamed him for his insistence that I had to desert the indoor decorating for the outdoor creosoting. Nevertheless, it reminds me that the old proverb, 'The more it changes, the more it stays the same,' is as undated as it ever was. The F/H/B could recall Mother painting the outside of their farmhouse and calling on the young boy-chap who worked there to hold the ladder steady whilst she tackled the upstairs windows. Clad in her workaday uniform of a cotton dress with a voluminous skirt, topped with a stout towser pinny, she missed her footing and slid down the ladder spot on into the lad's upstretched arms which shot straight up inside her skirt resulting in him clinging to her stays as they rolled together in the grass.

◦◇◆◇◦

Farmers can take over certain tasks in the spring, but outside of breeding that colt, training that sheepdog or handling the chain-saw, these little extras are disposed of with all possible speed, minus any embellishment. Chimneys are 'dealt with' rather than swept, by firing a gun straight up and bringing down the soot in a great black shower, from which Farmer walks away with only the whites of his eyes showing. The chimney over our solid-fuel Rayburn cooker caught fire one hot August morning, the flames sweeping across the old ceiling beam in the kitchen with a terrifying roar. Panic-stricken, I dialled 999 and the Fire Brigade arrived in minutes. The F/H/B was crossing a field looking at sheep, accompanied by one of our visitors, when they heard the fire engine roaring up the hill from Dulverton. 'Some poor sod's house is on fire,' the F/H/B said to his companion, only to find the appliance outside his own back door when he arrived home, and the kitchen filled with fire-fighters. Luckily the kitchen was situated at one end of our Devon longhouse and the walls were thick, the breakfast was already cooked, and the guests filed into the dining room with no knowledge of the pandemonium in the next room. All was tranquillity with 'May I pass you the prunes, my dear,' and, 'Have you noticed how overworked that little banty cock is in the yard? I think I'll have a word with Mr Huxtable after breakfast,' – Mr Huxtable, at that moment, had other things on his mind than overworked banty cocks, like assisting the fire-fighters, who all turned out to be familiar faces, the plumber, the saddler, the garage man and a couple of others. An axe was being wielded by one of them to chop out the offending beam where the fire had started, which, they reckoned, had been smouldering out of sight for a week, before finally busting out into flames. I managed to weave around the firemen and serve the ten guests their breakfasts, but then I panicked slightly as I remembered I did not possess an electric toaster, the bread always being toasted on the Rayburn fire. With hindsight, on that one eventful day, there is no doubt that the guests would have settled for plain bread and butter, but just at that crucial point it seemed imperative that they should not miss out on their breakfast toast. 'Don't put the fire out yet!' I implored, 'I got to do the visitors' toast!' The saddler, who was in charge, understood, and gave the order, 'Men, stand back,' he commanded, 'the lady got to do the frigging toast!' I unhung the long toasting fork from the wall, pronged the bread onto it, and toasted ten rounds with the firemen keeping careful watch lest the flames leapt out of control again. I arranged the slices of toast in their racks and carried them through to the dining room. 'Have you got company out there?' asked one elderly gentleman, 'I thought I heard voices.'

'Well, you could say that,' I answered, attempting to sound jauntily mysterious, before disappearing back to the scene of action, where everything appeared to be well under control, with the F/H/B putting the kettle on for a tea party with our rescuers.

Mercifully, the Rayburn fire was not thought to be dangerous, so was allowed to stay alight, although the whole massive chimney was exposed after the great oak beam had been backed away. Once we had cleared up the kitchen it was back to business as usual. Seemingly heard news of the fire on the grapevine and visited us that same evening. He looked in dismay at the great gaping hole where the chimney-breast had been. 'You'll never git no grub out of 'ee for a bit,' he forecast, 'you'll have to send all your folks home.'

'No need!' I told him, 'I've done dinner for ten right here tonight.'

Seemingly pondered deeply. 'You won't do it tomorrow night if the wind changes and there's downdraught down that gurt hole.'

'Not to worry,' I said, 'according to the weather forecast the wind'll stay the same for the rest of the week.'

Seemingly persisted. 'I'll tell you what, Missus, if it comes to snow you'll be up Shitters' Ditch.'

'Look,' I said, 'it's August 19th and I wouldn't say 'tis going to snow in the next day or two, so don't you worry your head about us.'

'Us'll see, us'll see,' rumbled our neighbour reaching for a glass of his favourite super-phosphate. 'You just mark my words.'

'Mark your words for what, you old fool?' I wanted to know.

'If I told you, you'd know as much as me,' he said, which was as good a let-out as any to close a conversation.

We awaited the insurance assessor, forearmed as to what to expect by one of our guests who was himself an insurance man.

'Don't give way,' he informed us, 'you'll be ending up with asbestos back behind and a false beam in front and they'll call it betterment and say you got to contribute out your own pocket, but tell 'em to get stuffed.' Which is exactly what the F/H/B did.

◇◇◆◇◇

Taking guests can be a real bonus as they come from all walks of life and give of their advice freely, quite apart from tackling the little repair jobs that never seem to get done. If they are doing outside jobs the F/H/B terms them good chaps, but if they tackle household jobs they're fit for nothing but tagging along behind a woman. Folks outside farming generally view it as a tranquil, idyllic lifestyle, never giving a thought to the numerous fiery issues that arise. It can be a roller-coaster in which Missus can, at times, achieve rapid promotion to M'lady status, and equally rapid demotion when Farmer's tractor gets a fit of the gripes and won't start, his hat's blown off in the wind, 'tis too foggy to hunt, and – wait for it – 'tis all her fault. M'lady status swiftly plummets, with Missus, her features arranged sorrowfully in acknowledgement of her man's suffering, stands there to give him somebody to swear at. If she can emphasise a bit by jumping up and down, so much the better, before dismissal comes with a curt 'you can be off now'.

Notwithstanding that repairs and make-do-and-mend have never taken priority in a farmhouse, the exact opposite can be said for the yard, where nothing, no matter how useless, is ever thrown out. Anything beyond repair and impossible to tie, stick or kick together has, for generations past, been carefully hoarded in old outbuildings, which, when finally overflowing with old oil lamps and tin buckets without handles would be boarded up never to see daylight again. Sometimes an attic in the house would be requisitioned, which, in the present day, would be turned into a bathroom, but back in years agone, Granfer would have protested vehemently that 'it ain't natural for water to travel h'wards', then, as an afterthought, declaring that he had not had a bath for sixty years and was lily white. If nature called at dead of night it meant dressing up in thorn-proof tweeds, and a chilly trek down the garden path to the privy. Once, when the tin roof blew off, Granfer fixed up an old black brolly, and, with the *Farmers' Weekly* in a biscuit tin, it was business as usual. Binder cord, and later, baler cord, is all carefully saved for its many uses and can, to this day substitute for braces and boot-laces and belts. Not matching baler cord, that might be thought effeminate, and sooner than have that damming label, Farmer would lace his boots with a bit of barbed wire.

Outfits were often completed with an ensemble known as Lord Carnarvon's livery, which comprised two corn bags, one worn across the shoulders, the other around the waist, tied on with binder cord, and guaranteed weatherproof.

Sheep's fleeces were often kept and stored in a little room known as the 'wool chamber', until the price went up, so there was usually a fleece on hand that could be used as upholstery, which was a grandiose word used to describe stuffing Granfer's old sagging armchair with something shaggy off a sheep. Cushions were stuffed with horsehair. Fresh horsehair. One old farmer even ordered his housekeeper to hack the mane and tail off his dead carthorse for the extra comfort of a few more cushions. Being a paid employee she was expected to do plenty beyond the normal call of duty and at the same time turn a deaf ear to neighbourly rumblings that if somebody stood in Farmer's yard at midnight and shouted 'Fire!', two heads would pop out the same window.

Housekeepers were always regarded with mistrust, not only because they smacked of sinfulness, but also they called housekeeping working for a living and expected a weekly wage on top of their keep. Finding a bride for Seemingly, our bachelor neighbour was uphill work all the way, as he made no effort to help himself, expecting a Marilyn Monroe lookalike, albeit with muscles, to land on his back doorstep as if by magic. His sentiments on women matched the F/H/B's when he proclaimed, 'I dunno, 'tis sposed to be easier to find a second-hand woman yerabouts than a second-hand horse, but you just show me where, Squire!'

I always had it in mind that a nice little widow-woman would suit Seemingly, but we had travelled that road on several occasions with no success whatsoever, whilst our neighbour thoughtfully philosophised that if a chap don't catch a woman in her widow's weeds then he's not likely to catch her at all. 'And I ain't never caught one yet,' he sadly mused once. 'Not in fifty-four years and it ain't as though I'm a bit seemingly particular.'

'You can't afford to be particular,' I told him. 'Not any more. You just got to grab what comes along and hope for the best.'

'Seemingly so,' agreed our neighbour. 'And I ain't exactly asking for the sun, moon and stars. All her got to do is handle a bale or two of hay, pick a chicken for dinner, mebbee take out a few pony trekkers to pay for her keep...' His voice trailed, then came back again. 'Her would have to be a maid with a fair-sized frame to be much use.'

'Not too big a frame,' interrupted the F/H/B. 'Costs too much to keep.'

Seemingly appeared not to be heeding, drifting off uncharacteristically into a little dream world of his own.

'Legs like shovel sticks,' he murmured. 'A frontside like a duchess and a backside like...'

'Stop it,' I ordered. 'That's enough of that sort of talk. What you want is a nice respectable little body that'll tidy your place up a bit. You too,' I added, casting my eyes over my neighbour's stringy frame encased in thick corduroys stiffened with wear, and his collarless shirt inherited from Grandad.

He leant forward confidentially and lowered his voice as though fearful of being overheard.

'Might seemingly happen sooner than you think, Missus.' He took a deep breath, 'Tomorrow I got a woman coming. For an interview.'

'Interview for what?' I queried. 'A bride?'

'No, you mazed fool. For a housekeeper.'

'You never advertised for a housekeeper!' The F/H/B was incredulous.

'No,' Seemingly said. 'Her did.'

'Did what?'

'Her advertised and I answered. Lookie.' He rummaged in his waistcoat top pocket and pulled out a crumpled newspaper clipping laying it carefully on the kitchen table. I snatched at it and read aloud 'Ladylike person seeks housekeeping situation with single gentleman, view to permanent residence. Great on T.L.C.'

'What's T.L.C?' The F/H/B wanted to know.

'To the best of my knowledge,' Seemingly answered in a man-of-the-world voice, ''tis tractors, lorries and cars.'

'You ain't got no car,' protested the F/H/B.

'I got me sheep wagon, same thing, got wheels, goes along the road. If her can drive a lorry, like her says, her can drive that one. And don't forget me tractor. Could be a useful maid, her could. The F/H/B still voiced doubts, looking again at the newspaper cutting. 'Her says ladylike person, you don't git many of they driving lorries and tractors. What you want is somebody that can skin a rabbit.'

Seemingly was not disposed to carry on the conversation, unbuttoning his waistcoat, hooking his fingers in his clip-on braces and rocking on his heels gently to and fro. 'Us'll see, Squire, us'll see,' was his parting shot. Before he left I offered to give his cottage a going-over before the new lady housekeeper arrived, and he accepted swiftly and gratefully.

The next morning I set off up the lane carrying a basket packed with scouring pad, disinfectant, polish, and two new yellow dusters. I let myself in through Seemingly's back door, recoiling slightly as I always did, at the sight that met my eyes. The long old farmhouse table was crowded with pans of milk from the Jersey cow, used crockery and baskets of eggs, whilst in the midst, a couple of Rhode Island Reds scratched with a confidence born of long experience. A third hen clucked contentedly from inside a large saucepan. The windowsill was crammed with purring cats sunning themselves, whilst a short queue of assorted tabbies waited hopefully on the flagstones underneath for a seat in the sun to be vacated. Beside the Rayburn cooker was Seemingly's armchair, with the seat missing, but with the requisite sheep's fleece stuffed in its place. On the wall, pendulum briskly swinging, hung Grandfather's old clock and I suffered my usual initial shock looking at it until I remembered he kept it 'one hower fast and ten minutes slow because 'tis good for me h'arithmetic.'

I rolled up my sleeves, propped open the back door with a tin bucket, and, seizing a broom addressed the cats and chickens in a voice that could be heard three fields away. 'Now then, you lot, outa it!'

Three days later Seemingly was back at our dinner table, which came as a surprise to us because by then we assumed the new housekeeper might be attending to his dinners. 'Her never stopped,' he told us dejectedly, 'too much of a lady for these parts. Talked just like what the Queen do.'

'What about the tractors, lorries and all that driving her was going to take on?' asked the F/H/B.

'Made out her didn't know nort about such things,' said Seemingly. 'Seems to me they'll tell any old tale to catch a man.'

'Seemingly,' I asked, 'I seem to recall in the past you – 'er – interviewed a couple of other ladies. What become of they?'

He pondered deeply. 'The first, as I recollect, was like one of they old sheep with a worm on the brain, tearing the place to pieces, seemingly a proper spendthrift, woulda had the shirt off a chap's back, that one.' He grimaced to himself, recalling the next one, 'Now her was builded the wrong way round, her had this frontside like a stallion and backside like…'

'That'll do,' I interrupted.

'I don't understand it, Maid,' he continued. 'After all, I ain't a bit particular.'

I felt a great surge of pity for our neighbour. He was a good chap and deserving of the love of a good woman. But where to find one? I had the glimmering of an idea that things might better fall into place if he could employ more of a helper than a housekeeper, a woman who could arrive early morning and work indoors and out, then return to her own home every evening. Perhaps such events would map their own course, and there might be a happy ending in sight.

Discussing my plan with Seemingly, at first he seemed dubious, pointing out that for a chap who had a cage, the bird was taking a long time to fly in. 'And another thing,' he went on, warming to his subject. 'I ain't fancying one of they au pair maids, us all know all they thinks about is sax.' It was pointless arguing that a glorious Nordic clone was hardly likely to grapple with our stringy old friend with a view to taking advantage of him. It became even more remote as the weeks slipped by and life for all of us went on much as usual. And then, out of the blue, we heard of a hefty, fourteen-stone, corduroy-clad, naily-booted all-rounder with a whinny that could be heard three fields away. She had a countrywoman's rosy cheeks and a bustling air of get-up-and-go. Furthermore, it was rumoured she was at an age when no good offer would be turned down, so her intentions, like Seemingly's, were strictly honourable. As she lived at home with her parents she would cycle to work everyday. By mutual agreement she was taken on a month's trial, and Seemingly appeared delighted at her performance. She milked the cow and fed the chickens and painted and papered and cooked and even turned up on Sundays. In fact it was quite touching to see the pair of them on their Sunday afternoon stroll across the turnip field with Seemingly pointing out all the finest specimens to his knowledgeable companion. At the end of the trial period the new housekeeper cycled up the road never to return. 'Whatever went wrong?' I demanded of our downcast neighbour, and he explained there was no way he could afford to keep her.

'I never seen a woman feed like it,' he said sadly, 'half a loaf of bread, two – three – lamb chops and a couple of pounds of tetties in one go. Too big a frame her had, cost too much to feed. Next time, Missus, when you be on the lookout for me, jus' make sure you pick one with a bit smaller frame. Not that I'm bit particular, you understand.'

'No,' I snapped, 'I don't understand, and I'm not likely to, the way you'm going on. Next time you can find your own maid.'

'It pays to remember,' said Seemingly, enunciating every word slowly, 'it pays to remember that a penny bun costs tuppence when there's two of 'ee.' There seemed to be no answer to that piece of logic. I had a feeling I had heard it somewhere before, probably from the F/H/B.

◇◇◆◇◇

Cats, Chat and Courting

If there was one thing the F/H/B could never abide, along with pigs and rice pudding, it was cats. Pigs, he would grudgingly concede, became passable once they land on a chap's plate, and, come to that, even rice pudding is likely to be a godsend to folks without teeth, but cats – 'cats be useless'. His philosophy was that there could well be rats in the feed shed, but a bag of Slaymore and a couple of borrowed terriers would work out a sight cheaper than keeping a cat on tinned chicken's innards.

For cat lovers it takes little effort on their part to turn a yard into something resembling a wildlife park. Cats breed non-stop from 1 February to 30 September. Cats swarm like monkeys over tractors, cars and anything that moves. I know of one such farm that displays a sign for the benefit of visitors, warning 'CATS. KEEP CAR WINDOWS SHUT', whilst on departure they are faced with 'STOP! Now check your car for cats!'

Cat lovers readily admit that their animals can inveigle themselves into the most hardened heart. Locals remember the touching posters along a certain stretch of road bewailing the loss of a runaway wife, together with the couple's cat. 'MISSING' read the first poster in large capitals. 'ONE WIFE. ONE CAT. REWARD FOR RETURN OF CAT'. This was followed by half a dozen other posters, planted in the roadside hedge at intervals for maximum impact, mindful of a Parish Council Election campaign.

The serious side to this, however, is that it is surprising how many defecting wives will leave their husbands, their home, their prized possessions, but never their cat – usually because they love it to bits, or, quite likely, because it is a final body blow in the break-up. One fighting couple who owned Herby, a three-legged cat, split up, with the wife staying on in the family home and the husband moving back into his parents' house. 'There I was,' he recalled, 'sleeping back in my own little room that I had as a boy, and, hell, did I hate it without Herby. I'd never have believed I could miss a cat so much.' Ten weeks later, reconciled, he moved back home with his wife.' It was worth putting up with her,' he confided, 'just to be back with Herby.'

At Chilcott we owned what I always believed to be a rarity, a ginger she-cat. As a kitten she had been taken to the local vet by a lady who had almost driven her car over the tiny thing in a thunderstorm. The local lady had been motoring across the moors, and rescued the drowning kitten from a puddle, more dead than alive. It appeared to have dropped from the sky, there being no habitation anywhere to be seen, and looked in urgent need of treatment. I happened to be visiting the vet's surgery a day or so later and was shown the little ginger kitten, still muddied with its coat sticking up in spikes like a hedgehog, and looking listless and quite poorly. So certain was the kindly vet that the kitten would survive that he commenced his sales-talk patter... 'He'll make a nice little ginger tom when he grows up. Great mousers and ratters ginger toms – reckon he'll be up and running by the end of next week – I mean, if you'd like to take the little chap you're welcome.' He was persuasive.

'Are you sure,' I wanted to know, 'about it being a tom-cat I mean?' The vet fixed me with the look of one whose knowledge has never before been challenged. 'You don't get ginger shes,' he said emphatically. 'Well only in rare cases and then they can be very valuable.'

'Right,' I said, 'I'll let you know. Got to ask the boss first.'

The boss was not impressed as we already had a Siamese cat that he had labelled useless, which had also been given to us, together with a box of apples. Knowing him to have been an expensive present to a friend, we soon found out why he was given away as the Siamese, aptly named Lucifer, appointed himself head-of-household and even gave the F/H/B his best shot, taking over his armchair and daring to be shifted. Their confrontations were awesome, usually emanating in the F/H/B snatching his cap off his head and swiping at the cat, who would howl threateningly back, fall off the chair and then grab his enemy with both paws round an ankle, his fearsome claws attempting to draw blood, a performance that did little to cement a friendly relationship between the two.

In view of all this, and the F/H/B not being a 'cat man' anyway, it took all my courage to broach the subject of taking on another cat. Luckily the vet himself happened to call and did all the persuading necessary to convince the F/H/B that a ginger tom-cat would be an asset to the yard. After he had gone, though, the F/H/B rounded on me, 'You and that vet be a conspiracy. I'll have that cat on one condition, and one condition only, and that is he never comes in this house. He'll be here to work, not like this other lazy bugger.' He shook the kitchen chair the Siamese was curled up on, but Lucifer clung tightly on, glaring up at his tormentor with malevolent blue eyes, and opening his month to release a screech so menacing I feared for my man's jugular. The vet told us he had named the ginger kitten Perdu, which he told us was French for lost. 'Lot of bloody nonsense,' scoffed the F/H/B. 'He'll be called Ginger and if he don't work he can go back to where he come from, and I'll say no more than that.'

Ginger was installed on a straw bed in the stable, where he lived for about a fortnight, but he was still a small and pathetic little creature and winter was coming on, so when he started to creep into the kitchen for a warm-up beside the Rayburn, even the F/H/B affected not to notice. I half expected the Siamese to show the intruder the outside door in no uncertain fashion, and he made it clear from the outset that he was very much in charge, a situation the little incomer accepted, wisely keeping a low profile as he gave the fiery Siamese a wide berth. The F/H/B noticeably mellowed when Ginger started work, the little cat even proudly carrying some of his mouse trophies indoors which the Siamese would pounce on and confiscate, devouring them with lip-smacking relish. Ginger was, after all, proving himself the asset that I had hoped for. Until the day, that is, the F/H/B encountered his mouse-catcher walking down the road from the next-door farm carrying a mouse in his mouth, and reports from our neighbours indicated he was actually spending some time there working in a rodent-infested shed, whilst, as the boss termed it, still on our pay-roll. Disloyal, he called it.

Howsoever, just as he was working himself into a lather, a new situation manifested itself, taking the heat out of Ginger's defection to next door, but replacing it with a bigger problem. It seemed that the little cat's ever-increasing girth was not due solely to mouse-intake, but something more akin to misconduct. Our ginger tom was pregnant. The F/H/B looked all set to have a seizure when I told him, but I attempted to defuse the situation by remembering the vet saying ginger shes were so rare as to be worth a bit of money. 'Right, then,' said the ever-practical farmer. 'He can buy the cat back and us'll be done with it.'

'I can't,' I told him, standing my ground. 'He's part of the family. I don't want to part with him – her – it.'

The F/H/B, he of the short fuse, was becoming irate. 'So what's the sense in you telling me that thing's worth money' – pointing to Ginger, by now sitting in his own little cardboard box in the warm, happy and briskly washing – the F/H/B warmed to this theme. 'Investments is supposed to be turned over, not stop static, so have some sense for once, Maid – us don't want a heap of bleddy old kittens about the place. And'... the voice shot up an octave, ''tis all your fault anyways.'

I decided to ring the vet there and then, telling him his ginger tom-cat was pregnant. He was incredulous, reiterating that he had never before come across an all-ginger she but yes, he had made enquiries and they were not, he admitted, as rare as he first thought, and er-er, probably had no more value than any other cat. I gleefully recounted the conversation to the F/H/B who, by now, was showing difficulty in reconciling to a pregnant ginger tom who worked next door. Little more was left to be said on the matter, and I began, quietly, to look forward to the kittens being born, something we had never had before. I wondered who Daddy might be, and finally my trail of thought made me think of a familiar old tabby known locally as the Opportunist, who spread himself fairly thin on the ground with occasional visits to farms over what we all believed to be a wide area. He never outstayed his welcome, but that might have been due to some inbuilt premonition that a permanent home could have cost him his manhood. The Opportunist knew his territory and would often show up at lambing time when a farmer's wife, spending a quiet moment in the orchard sitting on a fallen tree trunk, would be bottle-feeding a couple of lambs. She would never be too surprised when the old tabby would dive over the hedge, give a loud miaow in greeting, then place himself with an accuracy born of long practice, directly under the lamb's bottle and catch all the drips of milk. The next morning he usually presented himself in the shippon as Farmer milked the house cow into a tin bucket, every now and then twisting the cow's titty to direct a stream of warm, creamy milk into the Opportunist's open mouth. Then he would wander off, never staying long enough to be a nuisance, to visit another area. We found out that originally he was a feral cat who was given a home by a kindly couple in Dulverton, and he lived with them for four or five years before suddenly leaving his warm, cosy home to return to life in the wild. Although he visited his former home and friends from time to time, he preferred the gipsy life, and as he was still a full-blown tom-cat, it was almost a certainty that he would have fathered Ginger's kittens.

Our little cat's girth broadened daily, the vet telling me the gestation period for cats being fifty-eight days, and I found myself counting them off daily, and hoping Ginger would not give birth in some silent, secret place where we would never find them. My fears turned out to be needless. I was rolling out pastry on the kitchen table when she hurtled in through the window, landing on the flagstones before me, looking directly up at me and wailing a long-drawn-out miaow I had never heard before, then she turned and waddled towards the back door. I registered that it was odd she should jump in through the window and then rush straight to the back door to be let out. I opened the door and the little cat hopped down the two steps into the yard, ran the distance of half a gunshot, then came back distressed, and wailed plaintively again. It seemed almost as though she was waiting for me to follow her. As she led off again, racing as fast as her increased girth would allow, I trailed her, straight to the stables, up the steps to the loft and over a mound of loose hay where Ginger disappeared into a carefully scratched out nest, like an igloo. She flopped into it, never taking her great amber eyes off me and let out another gurgling cry from one end whilst lifting a back leg to let out a tiny ginger kitten from the other end. She settled then, and I watched her give birth to three kittens in all, two gingers and a tortoiseshell. She was proud of her family; a succession of visitors climbed the rickety ladder to the stable loft in the ensuing weeks, including even the F/H/B, who summed up the little family in one word –'time-wasters'.

Every year thereafter Ginger produced her litter of three kittens, always the same make-up of two gingers and one tortoiseshell, and each year we went through the same routine, sometimes in the stables, once or twice in the pigs' house and many times in the hay or straw barn, and without exception she demanded that I be there.

Once was on a Saturday morning, which was changeover day for the visitors, when I heard her about-to-give-birth wail out in the yard. I was making beds and without a minute to spare, and, to my shame whenever I thought about it afterwards, I leaned out of the window and shouted to her to go away. She looked up, wailing, pleading with me to go down and follow her. I steeled myself to go on with the bed-making and the next time I checked from the window there she was lying amongst the stones in the yard giving birth to the first kitten. Shamed, I rushed downstairs and scooped up the kitten and let Ginger lead me to the nest she had prepared in the barn, staying with her until she was happily settled with her three new babies. It took no time at all, but although she had obviously squared-up to motherhood, she still needed that extra security in her insistence that I shared the birth with her. The F/H/B was less than enthusiastic. 'Lot of bleddy nonsense,' he grumbled, 'no need for any of it – I ain't keeping any of that lot and 'tis up to you to find places for 'em, and if you don't there's going to be the biggest bleddy row us ever had.' I believed him, because he would consider kittens to be passengers, and farmers never carry pets or passengers no matter who or what.

I recalled a neighbouring farmer with a magnificent herd of beef cattle who was in great demand to sell to private buyers. On one such occasion a farmer from Leicester arranged to collect a dozen of the beasts and he was being taken round the cattle sheds by the vendor to select the animals, when they were unaccountably joined by the farmer's wife. Now wives are definitely persona non grata when their husbands are cattle dealing, their place is indoors getting the tea, whether it's in Leicester or the West Country or even, quite likely in Timbuktu. Howsoever, on this particular day the wife joined the party, unannounced and ignored, trotting quietly behind as the visitor from Leicester singled out the animals that caught his eye. The reason for the wife's presence became apparent when he decided on a particularly outstanding bullock, one that stood stock still as she rubbed its ears.

'Not this one,' she said, tugging on her husband's sleeve. 'Please, not this one.'

'Quiet, woman,' he growled.

She persisted, tearfully, 'But that's Muffin!'

Sensing the discord the Leicester man attempted to cool the situation, after all there were plenty to choose from.

'Don't worry, Missus,' he said, 'I'll pick another.'

The farmer seller was forceful and adamant.

'If that's the bullock you want, then that's the one you take,' he added scribbling in his notebook.

The wife squared her shoulders and made her stand. 'If Muffin goes, I go.'

'Well, shove off, then,' said the uncaring farmer, leaning forward to mark Muffin with a yellow marking stick, thus sealing his destiny.

This sort of attitude in our country, churlish as it seems, pales in comparison to countries further afield. It is said that in the Afghan hills the farmers brand their wives along with their sheep, using the self-same branding iron. Their views on pets and passengers are likely to be in line with our own, and, they like the F/H/B, would definitely include a severe embargo on litters of kittens. In a way I was almost surprised that Ginger's kittens had been allowed to survive, but my promise that they would all be found jobs by the time they were eight or nine weeks old probably had some bearing on that matter. The key word here was 'jobs'; the F/H/B could not believe that anybody could ever house a cat just for the pleasure of its company.

As the kittens grew, progressing from opening their eyes at ten days old, to moving around and eating the tiny mice their mother caught for them, I realised they were hardly lookalikes for the perfect specimens pictured on cards and calendars. The biggest of the three was a rangy ginger tom who looked like he had been put together in a hurry. His neck was skinny, and his tail was bent in the middle, which gave him a sad looking physique, altogether out of touch with his fancy to be the bullyboy of the three. The second kitten was a pale, rather faded looking tortoiseshell with a loud, wheezy chest to serve as a warning hooter to rodents a gunshot away. The third was the best looking by far, a deep red cat with dark stripes and an immaculate white front. Sadly, he had one good eye and another not-so-good eye.

I decided to advertise the kittens in the local newsagent's, and I wrote out a card accordingly, which read simply, 'Good homes wanted for lovely ginger kittens.' I showed it to the F/H/B who sniffed scornfully, 'You'm asking for trouble,' he said. 'The weights and measures chap'll be after you.'

'What the heck's that got to do with cats?' I enquired, irritated at the look of smug satisfaction on his face.

'Misrepresentation,' he cackled. ''Cos there's nort "lovely" as you calls it, about that lot.'

'I think you're talking about Trade Descriptions, not weights and measures,' I said coldly. Nonetheless, once he was out of sight I crossed out 'lovely' and substituted 'useful'.

On my way to the newsagent's I encountered the local policeman and thought of trying to get a kitten a mousing job at the Police Station. The policeman lifted his cap and scratched his shock of dark hair thoughtfully. ''Tis all according,' he said cautiously. 'Is this cat likely to be conscientious in the pursuit of his duty, good in all gears, like?' Mindful of the Trade Descriptions, I could not, in all honesty, guarantee it. I could sense he was fast losing interest.

Once back home I remembered it was Tuesday and the Tallyman was due to call. He came round once a month, bringing clothes and household goods, a boon to country-folk, not only because of the useful goods he brought, but all the news he collected along his route. I cooked some nice fresh trout with butter and almonds for our lunch, and afterwards when he was nicely relaxed I asked if the would like to do me a favour and take home one of the kittens. He leapt out of his chair and headed for the door faster than I ever remembered, banging it behind him, then reopening it to yell, 'Thanks for the trout, misses but one trout don't equal a cat, no way!'

My advertisement seemed to be going nowhere when a lady with a small fat boy dressed in a cowboy outfit, turned up to enquire about the kittens. 'My little boy is very interested in animals,' cooed Mummy. 'I ain't your little boy, I'm the Sheriff,' announced the child; pushing past me to where the cats were playing on the lawn. 'Howdy, ugly,' he greeted Squint Eye, then passed on to Bent Tail. 'Har, har, har, look at that, his tail's bin through the mangle.' He clicked his six-gun at Wheezy's chest, 'Listen, Ma, sounds like this 'uns ready for the last round-up.' He thrust the gun at Mummy and peeped under each kitten's tail, then let out a squawk. 'Hey, Ma, they still got their conkers! Where's me gun, I'll shoot 'em off!'

'Darling,' said Mummy, 'don't be so assertive or the pussy cats won't like you at all.'

'Don't care,' shouted the cowboy, 'I don't want one of these funny old cats anyway. I wanna great big horse and a great big dog and a great big motor car and...'

'Yes, of course you do, darling,' said Mummy soothingly.

'And I'm not your darling, I'm the Sheriff – Now say it, Ma.'

'Yes, right you are, Sheriff,' said Mummy loudly and obediently.

Then, turning to me, 'Justin is such a good boy.'

The good boy stamped a foot and burst into noisy tear. 'I just told you, I'm the Sheriff and I wanna be called Sheriff.' He aimed a kick at Mummy's leg as she put her arms lovingly round her child, gathering him close, obviously a tried and tested format to take the force out of the punches he was then aiming at her. She turned to me. 'I'm so sorry,' she said, 'I think Justin – I mean the Sheriff – seems to have changed his mind about having one of your kitties. I'm afraid we've taken up a lot of your time, although living out here you're probably quite pleased to see someone come in.'

I did not offer tea; the thought of a minute longer than necessary in the company of that child would have been a severe test of temperament on my part, and to have let one of Ginger's kittens go to such a home would have been unthinkable. As Mummy and the Sheriff disappeared out into the yard, I could still hear his screeches fading into the distance, 'I wanna great big horse and a great big dog and…'

The next enquiry for a kitten came unexpectedly from Nellie and George across the valley. They turned up on the back doorstep, having seen my advertisement in the newsagent's. It was a warm day, but whilst George was lightly clad, Nellie wore her sheep-dipping uniform of long brown overcoat, naily boots, and matching brown felt hat. Nellie didn't waste time with prelimaries. 'You got cats,' she stated. 'Why the hell you never told your neighbours before sticking adverts in that old biddlehead's shop winder I'll never know.' I apologised. I had no idea Nellie might be wanting a kitten and we were hardly on the same wavelength when it came to discussing anything other than sheep.

'Right then,' said Nellie, anxious to get on with the business – 'Let's see if there's ort worth having.'

She scrutinised the three candidates for a home before pointing a long, skinny finger at Bent Tail. 'Us'll have 'ee,' she decided. 'Best of a poor bunch. T'other two's no good, bleddy liabilities they'd be. Month's trial. I ain't taking a pig in a poke. Delivered,' she added, which was fair enough as they had walked from across the valley as neither she nor George could drive a car. I felt obliged to demur over Nellie's demand for a month's trial for a kitten. Even a guaranteed pony merited only a week's trial at the most, and a buyer would be paying good money for it, whilst the kitten was free. I pointed out to

Nellie that in a month's time the kitten would still be at the learning stage, it could hardly be assessed at such a young age.

'Suit your bleddy self,' said Nellie in her strident voice, 'take it or leave it.'

I capitulated, as we all did when Nellie was in charge.

'Look,' I said. 'I'll run you both home now in the car and you can take the kitten with you.' 'Thank you very much m'dear,' said George who spoke so rarely that he quite startled me. 'My feet be aching from walking over, leave alone getting back.' 'Nope,' said Nellie firmly, adjusting her felt hat squarely on her head and giving George a shove towards the door, 'c'mon you lazy little bugger, git marching.'

'I got the wrong boots on fer walking,' protested George.

'And whose fault is that?' Nellie enquired pitilessly. 'You shoulda thought of that when you was putting 'em on, not now when you'm a donkey ride away. Anyways, exercise'll do you a bit of good, you forgets 'tis me who tackles all the work home. Now, get moving up that bleddy road.' Then, turning to me, 'And if that cat ain't in my place by seven o'clock tonight you can stick the little bugger where the monkey stuffs 'ees nuts.' And Nellie thumped her way out through the back door and strode purposefully up the hill, George, with his aching feet, tagging manfully along in her wake.

Three weeks passed before Nellie, long brown overcoat, felt hat as before, presented herself on the doorstep again. 'You can come and collect thik cat,' she said. 'Got no light home last night, the little bugger pee'd all over me oil lamp. Shan't keep 'ee.' There was no arguing with Nellie, which is why Bent Tail returned home to us to rejoin his brothers. There were no further offers of homes or jobs for the little family, which is why they all stayed at Chilcott and lived happily ever after, so to speak. The only one who was not happy was the F/H/B who I thought was likely to bust a gut every time he encountered them. Particularly when they all crept indoors through the winter and took up poll positions in front of the Rayburn, with the Siamese lording it over the lowly gingers from a cushion on the top left-hand corner of the cooker. Every night, at bed-time, the F/H/B would seize the long-handled sweeping brush and broom them all out of the back door into the yard, a routine they must have all recognised, together with the words, 'Right then, you've had the day off now you can bleddy well start to work.' They were often less than enthusiastic about their despatch and I remember one night when Archie dodged back in, only to be deftly fielded out again with the broom. I told the F/H/B that it was just as well Archie had a sense of humour, and he unexpectedly agreed, adding that he could hear him laughing as he shot across the yard.

Other than the kitchen, the cats were barred from the rest of the farmhouse as I was determined they should not roam upstairs and discover the comfort of visitors' beds. Even so, one or another would occasionally evade my strict security but I would propel them back down so fast their paws scarcely touched the stairs. Taking visitors made it essential that the animals knew their boundaries. Once, when I showed some visitors to their room, my eyes riveted on a telltale round hump in the middle of the bed, mercifully concealed under the quilt. As soon as the guests returned to their car to collect their luggage I whipped back the quilt and exposed Squint Eye, curled up fast asleep. I helped him make a hurried exit down the back stairs.

A more harrowing experience happened one Sunday afternoon when I was expecting a honeymoon couple to arrive. The bridegroom had telephoned his booking, telling me that he and his fiancée were to be married on the Saturday and would spend their honeymoon at Chilcott for a week. His bride, however, had no idea where he was taking her; it was all going to be a big surprise. He sounded loving and considerate, and I found myself chuckling along with him at the secrecy. They would be driving from Kent and would arrive on Sunday in time for tea. I gave him directions for reaching Chilcott from Dulverton, and I wished him a good journey with fine weather. It was not to be. Although it was mid-summer, Sunday was more like November: cloudy, dark, and with continuous heavy rain, Tiverton rain, as we call it. In most countries there can be depressions which last for up to four hours, in Ireland there is a lot of rain which accounts for the Emerald Isle, and there is Scottish mist and coastal drizzle, but nowhere is there rain like Tiverton rain. It is not the gentle rain of spring, it is not even insidious, it is not a thunder shower, it is heavy, slanting, torrential rain that never stops. It is Tiverton rain. That Sunday it beat across our yard, ponding up at the bottom and blocking the drains and never letting up.

I had prepared the four-poster room for the honeymooners, which was by far the most impressive of the six letting rooms. The bedcover, valance, curtains and kidney-shaped dressing table were all draped in pale blue satin cotton with a little sprigged floral design. The bed had been bought for £12 at a farm sale but the cost of the drapes and matching curtains had run into hundreds, which at that time I could ill afford. Howsoever, looking at it that Sunday it seemed so right for a romantic couple that it all had to be worth every penny. I arranged a bowl of pink roses from the garden on the dressing table, then went down and opened the front door to check on the weather. As I did so, one of the ginger cats shot past me and ran straight up the stairs, carrying a mouse in his mouth. I just spotted the cat's tail disappearing into the open door of the honeymooners' bedroom. At the same time a car turned into the yard with the young couple inside. The driver parked as far from the house as seemed possible, which ensured its passengers a soaking walk across the yard to the front door, which seemed to take forever. I waited for them, watching the bride teeter on tiny, tortuous steps through the racing rivulets in her champagne-coloured shoes with stiletto heels that had patently not been designed for an assault course. She looked neither to the right nor the left, a dark-haired pretty girl who was not, it must be said, looking very cheerful at that particular moment. Her bridegroom locked the car and caught up with her, attempting to take her arm, but she impatiently shook him off. She arrived in the doorway with her pale blue silk suit drenched and her wet hair pressed against her neck. Her first words were not encouraging.

'We were doing well until we ran into all this rain, and it took us two hours to find this place and we were running out of petrol, and just look at me!' The bridegroom gave a nervous twitch that passed for a smile. 'I 'er – I'm afraid I lost your excellent directions for finding you, and, 'er, well, I didn't know it would be in the country, well, not to this extent. I thought there would be signposts, and 'er well, you know, lampposts and things…' His voice trailed vaguely away, an earnest young man blinking behind thick, rain-spotted glasses. The bride directed at him a look best described as baleful. I attempted to soothe matters by suggesting I showed them to their room where they could shower and change and by then tea and cream scones would be ready for them in the sitting room, where, although it was meant to be summer, a log fire was burning, an attempt to cheer up a depressing day. As we went upstairs we met

Mr Slick on his way down. I had momentarily forgotten him with his mouse, and I could only hope he had already devoured it. As we entered the bedroom the bridegroom said appreciatively, 'This really looks very nice, don't you think, darling?' His bride gazed dismally through the window at the rain sweeping across the fields.

'It's a farm!' she said accusingly. 'You know I can't stand cows and pigs and things.'

'Sweetheart,' said her new husband reasonably, 'I'm sure it's only a teeny farm with teeny animals, and you'll love it.' He put a reassuring arm round her shoulders as the leaden skies emptied their load over Chilcott with redoubled force. It seemed ever darker and I switched on the bedroom light to cheer it all up a bit. It illuminated the kidney dressing table, where, hauling itself up one of the drapes, slowly and painstakingly, was one of the teeny animals in the shape of a very small field mouse. The bride spotted it at the same time and let out a scream that must have penetrated the stained-glass windows of Dulverton All Saints' Church three miles away. Turning, she clattered out through the door down the stairs and out into the yard in the torrential rain, running until she reached their car, struggling to wrench open the door. It was locked, and the new wife was left standing outside, still screaming and kicking the door with her high-fashion shoes, whilst the bridegroom stammered his apologies to me. I felt sorry for the bespectacled young man who had booked the surprise honeymoon, and who was about to realise that it was probably to be the shortest honeymoon in history, and also the last big decision he would ever make in married life. I sighed for them both as I stood in the rain and gave them a wave as their car finally roared up the road at high speed. Nobody waved back. I went back indoors, searched for Mr Slick and extracted him from a line of cats huddled against the Rayburn. I was marching him up the stairs to the four-poster room to finish his work when a wave of sentimentality overcame me, and I hustled him off back to the kitchen. I found the little mouse still engulfed in the drapes of the dressing table, small and frightened and shaking. I carried it downstairs and dropped it off in the garden. It may have been grateful, or, on the other hand, it may not. Not in that rain.

∘◇◆◇∘

Make no wonder the F/H/B always reckoned he should hang a sign over the front door at Chilcott, reading for the benefit of new visitors, 'You should have been here last week,' the meaning being that this week it's pouring with rain, whereas last week we all benefited from a couple of sunny days. People often arrive on holiday saying, 'Does it always rain here?' and my stock answer is always, 'You shoulda been here last week.'

Taking round the visitors' morning teas taught me a lot on how to evade unwanted questions on the weather, and now I'm as devious as any politician with answers that are really not answers at all, if you get my meaning. The regular guests soon cottoned on to my meteorological forecasts, knowing that when I told them, 'Oh, 'tis one of they old Exmoor days,' they might as well pull up the blankets and settle in bed for the day. Torrents of rain merited an optimistic, ''T'won't be long before you see across the yard,' or, shifting the onus onto another person, 'The postman says 'twill clear drekly,' drekly being dialect for soon, but actually meaning any time from next Christmas to next Easter, which ever comes last. One couple declared that I answered their question on the state of the weather with, 'Elvis Presley's died,' which reminded them for ever that Elvis died on a wet day in August.

Visitors often enquire of the locals for a weather outlook, and one couple, arriving back at Chilcott after spending their evening drinking in the local pub, with the oldest inhabitant, had memorised his answer to their question on the weather. They did so because (a) it seemed a bizarre forecast for August. And (b) after asking him to repeat it four times they gave up. They were word-perfect as they sat in the kitchen sipping their nightcap of Famous Old Whisky, and repeated to the F/H/B. ''Tis going to rain snow.' They paused, then enunciated once more. ''Tis going to rain snow. That's exactly how he said it. We know it's lousy but it is August, and for God's sake, surely not snow?'

They had to wait for the F/H/B to recover from his guffawing and knee-slapping mirth before he informed them, 'You got it all wrong – you buggers might be wise men where you come from, but down here you ain't got a bleddy clue. What Fat Bacon Charlie said was, '''Tis going to rain, dost' thou know.'' He never mentioned snow, not the way you'n thinking of it. He said s'now – cut it short like.'

'Abbreviation!' interjected the visitor. The F/H/B raised his glass and studied the whisky before saying. 'You call it what you like, and me and Fat Bacon'll call it what us like. Same thing, either way.'

'Hear, hear,' said the visitors, raising their glasses.

Visitors, however much we unkindly laugh at their attempts to understand our dialect, are not the only ones confused by it, as it tends to vary every few miles. When we moved to Chilcott from North Devon, a mere 27 miles in distance, we crossed the border into West Somerset where, for all we understood, conversations could have been conducted in Serbo-Croat. Auntie Dolly and Auntie Julie from Higher Chilcott paid us a visit on our first day in residence, the two little salt-of-the-earth elderly sisters each dressed in black with their identical brown boots. Auntie Julie, who told us she had lived away for some time working as a lady's maid, was the spokeswoman who handled the introductions. 'We are here to greet you,' she announced forwardly. 'I am Auntie Julie and this is my sister, Auntie Dolly, and it would please us if you call us that. We are here to help you in any way we can.' I called out to the F/H/B to come in from the yard, and, introductions over, we all had tea together. It was the first of many such occasions, either in our house or theirs. I soon observed that when one, or both of the sisters arrived wearing their best brown boots they had come to tea, whilst in their second-best black boots, it was usually to tell us a bit of local gossip or that one of their vast number of distant cousins had died. Because of the dialect difference between Devon and Somerset it took us some time to get to grips with the news-flashes, although we found Auntie Julie the clearer of the two because she had left the area for a while. Howsoever, with the two both talking at once, it was important to concentrate to get the gist of their conversations, together with masculine and feminine in a glorious mish-mash, as when they told us of a visit from the man from the Ministry (of Agriculture). 'He come to the door and then us took her up the field to see the yaws (sheep) and when us got back her had a cup of tea along wi' us.' We learnt from that that the masculine 'he' would only ever be used once, in the first reference, thereafter it translated into 'her'. But, if the visitor had been a woman, 'her' would have been eliminated in favour of 'she', as in, 'Us took she up the field' – etc.

It is a wonder to me that, what with the rain and the language hiccup, some enterprising soul does not set up that old stalwart advertised by Continental hotels for when the weather is bad: 'No-frills language courses.' The National Park is the body that springs to mind, who might start by bringing out a small dictionary of useful words and phrases, on the lines of 'Get tuned-in to Exmoor'. As with the foreign manuals, the aim would be to give information and 'some forms of courtesy'.

A *Rough Guide* might commence with:

Greeting	**'Ow be 'ee?'**
(As with some foreign languages 'H' is rarely pronounced)	
Yes	**'Tis all according**
No	**'Tis all according**
Drunk	**Cidered-up**
Off your legs	**Barrowed home**
(in wheelbarrow)	
Off your head	**Mazed as a brush**
Nutter	**Doughbake**
Unwell	**Touch of the nadgers**
Unwell	**Touch of the leurgy**
Something	**Ort**
Nothing	**Nort**
Going to bed	**Roost**
Flirtatious	**Horsing**
Slim	**Skintered**
Sensible knickers	**Britches**
Male, non-macho	**Half-knack**
Teenager	**Boy-chap**
Morning-after feeling	**Head like a thicket**
A bit of a go-er	**Dab hand at the rising trot**

After a few pages of basic words, a few conversation openers might prove useful, particularly on market day:
''Ow's yer grass?'
'What sort of worm drench/udder cream do you use?'
'You keep ferrets?'

'Well Done!' Depending on the inflection used, from praise to heavy sarcasm, from downing a pint of cider in one, to falling in a nettle bed.

With so many variations of dialect there are inevitably those who resist slotting into a single category. Uncle Percy (Auntie Dolly's and Auntie Julie's youngest brother, at eighty, still referred to as The Boy) would actually manage a 'yes', but pronounced it 'yum', whilst the Exmoor windsucker never uses words at all, substituting a sharp intake of breath, again with multiple inflections.

Perhaps the final advice in the *Rough Guide* should be from the F/H/B with his invaluable, 'If there's ort you don't understand just keep nodding yer head!'

◇◇◆◇◇

If conversation is difficult with 'foreigners' from other parts of Britain it could be well nigh impossible for Continentals visiting Exmoor. It can be worrying to read in a local newspaper that one or other of our villages has been 'twinned' with a counterpart abroad. Nothing could be more calculated to make our Exmoor man square his trustworthy shoulders, clamp his check cap firmly on his head and straighten his 'EAT BRITISH BEEF' T-shirt than the threat that his patch of the moor might be invaded in an 'exchange' with a foreign farmer. He strongly suspects that all the chaps be after is the womenfolk and once they land in the West Country they'll carry on like old rams with a worm on their brain. He fears them not, be they hefty, lederhosen-clad Germans sporting jaunty little hats with tom-fool feathers, nor graceful, perfumed Italians with brooding eyes; our man defies competition in his stripy braces, flies and naily boots laced with baler cord. Not matching. That would be sinking to their level. Neither does he fear a swarthy brigand, pedigree unknown, in tight, narrow trousers, swirling a full-length black opera cloak lined with red satin and a black sombrero tipped over a moustachioed face. He may even picture him, sleek and sophisticated, crossing the farm yard in exaggerated strides like a ballet dancer, leaping lightly on to the dung heap in shiny patent shoes and rendering an aria from La Traviata, before disappearing into the hen house to sip a glass of red wine.

None of this concerns our man because he is only too aware that Exmoor women are unlikely to be swept off their welly boots by marauding foreigners. If courtship is involved they are conditioned to one conducted with more caution than verve, one where they are regarded as a possible stable-mate more than an object of desire.

Countrymen are wholesome, displaying an unhurried approach to wedlock; once they have selected their chosen mate they winter her, summer her, and winter her again. The F/H/B and I pursued this leisurely course but I was not aware at the time that I was actually sitting a series of little exams that he had set me on account of my smallness of stature. Farmers generally prefer a maid carrying a bit of flesh, and he secretly worried I might not be up to all the jobs required. Therefore he encouraged me to cart bales of hay, 'preferably one in each hand,' he told me afterwards, 'and I could see you couldn't manage that, but you was fly on your feet and went double-quick, so that made up for it!' Then there was docking a sheep with one hand and rolling a fag with the other (the fag was for him), taking off a lamb and being able to do a bit of nursing if he ever got cidered-up. It seemed that I passed my final exam with flying colours – farmers prefer their Missus to be two eggs short of a dozen, because, they maintain, there are two things to beware of and those are intelligent pigs and intelligent women – 'you can't keep neither in their sty, they always want to see what's out on the other side.'

Planning a wedding is fraught with problems, mainly because there is no such thing as a convenient time in the farming world. There's lambing and tilling, hay harvest and corn, and before a maiden can say 'wedding bells', the bullocks are back in the sheds and the hunting season commences. The agenda is relentless. Howsoever, one of our neighbours managed to plan his wedding with a package that crammed the whole caboosh into one single weekend, with his stag night on Friday, wedding Saturday, honeymoon Sunday, and back home shearing sheep (with the new bride catching and tying wool) on Monday. He even found time to add to the presents list with his own essentials headed with a set of drain rods and a roll of barbed wire. With such a tight schedule guests might have expected the ceremony to be timed right to the minute, but by then the bridegroom decided he needed to relax a little, and headed, with his best man, for the village pub. He was still relaxing there half an hour after he should have declared his vows, leaving the parson and the wedding guests, including the bride's mother, who was not best pleased, adrift in church, whilst the bride's beribboned car cruised in circles round the village square to the cheers of the onlookers.

A one-day honeymoon is often considered quite long enough for a countryman who does not rate holidays high on his list of priorities. In fact I know of one strawberry grower in Combe Martin who told his bride they would have to go away separately as there was no way they could both be away together. She took him at his word and booked a week in Spain with a girlfriend whilst he sulked at home, unaware of the old Spanish proverb 'Keep her at home with a broken leg.' Which makes our menfolk appear manifestly benevolent.

Although customs have become slightly more relaxed since I was first wed, countrymen still have that inbuilt machismo that insists their wives stay at home and minister to their every need. I well remember the F/H/B's bachelor cousin dropping in on us one teatime just as he was getting ready to go to a meeting. He had changed into his suit and I was polishing his black shoes and could not resist drawing Cousin John's attention to the wifely duty I was carrying out, saying, there, if he had a wife he would get his shoes cleaned. He looked at me steadily over his teacup and said deliberately, 'If I had a missus I'd expect my shoes cleaned and ready, not left 'til the last minute!'

'Yeah,' said the F/H/B, 'remember that next time, Maid. Cleaned and ready!'

Cleaning shoes is small fry compared to the workload carried by some wives. On the opposite side of the moor to us is a fair-sized farm where, by mutual agreement, the wife is first up every morning, racing out to milk the house cow and feed the calves and chickens before returning indoors to find her man seated on the old kitchen settle, awaiting her return. The conversation, which he hilariously recounts now and again in the pub, never varies.

'Cup of tay, Maid.'

She hustles to the Rayburn, slams on the kettle, then carries him his tea.

'Bit of toast, Maid.'

Three rounds of toast are thickly buttered and carried over to Farmer.

Then, finally. 'Boots, Maid.'

She picks up the naily boots and exchanges them for his slippers. He reaches for his cap on the peg above and crams it on his head, ready for work. He is philosophical over his delayed arrival downstairs in the morning and discusses it openly. 'Ain't the time a fellow gets up, 'tis what he does afterwards. You see, m'dears, 'tis like this, if the good Lord had intended I got up in the morning He'd have giv'd me the strength to do it. But He ain't, He've giv'd it to her instead.'

We all were aware that every day the couple's routine never varied. The wife helped out twice daily with jobs that had become her own, including never missing milking the house cow. The F/H/B swore that with her tough physique and massive hands she could milk the cow in two minutes flat by ignoring the conventional four titties and simply wrapping her whopping hands round the whole of the cow's udder and giving just one almighty squeeze which would whoosh a couple of gallons straight into the bucket without the time-consuming preamble of dealing with each individual titty.

Although routines such as this are commonplace among the locals, incomers, such as our neighbours Richard and Patricia expressed amazement at what they considered to be abnormal indulgence of our menfolk. Looking at it from their angle, it probably was a severe culture shock for a couple from town, totally unconnected with the countryside, to discover a lifestyle so alien to the one they had led all their lives, patriarchal rather than matriarchal. Patricia, who, I discovered, prided herself on her diplomacy in dealing with the natives, confessed to finding our menfolk "Er – rather Victorian. I really don't think more educated – that is,' she added hastily, 'more urban women would not put up with them for long.' As this was said in the F/H/B's hearing it met with a swift response. 'They can please their bleddy selves,' he said. 'If all they wants is yes-men, then that's all they bleddy deserve.'

Patricia looked nettled and this proved the start of many such exchanges between the two of them. 'Me and her don't get on too well,' the F/H/B would chortle, squaring up for the next round. How two peasants, scratching around for tuppence, could live in Chilcott, a fifteen-room farmhouse, complete with well and a witches' stand, must have been a source of speculation to our aristocratic new neighbours who themselves moved to a country cottage from – in their own words – a fairly modest, detached suburban house. Patricia's curiosity manifested itself one day when she came in through our front door (she normally entered by the back door), and glanced up the wide staircase.

'To whom does this place belong?' she enquired.

'Us.'

'Yes, yes, my dear, I know you live here, but to whom does it actually belong?'

'It's ours!'

'Is that really so?' went on the plummy tones, disbelievingly. 'I thought you must be running it for, you know, someone else...'

The F/H/B appeared in the doorway, catching the tail end of the conversation, and rounded on Patricia, a man with a short fuse. 'And what's all that supposed to be about?' he demanded. 'I'm danged if you wouldn't make a helluva good prison wardress, the way you carries on – call yourself well-bred? I don't call you bleddy well-bred!'

The response came back even plummier.

'Well Ai don't call you very well bred, Arthur.'

'Ar, but I don't pretend to be!' snarled the F/H/B, slamming the door behind himself as he left.

'Have a cup of tea, Patricia,' I offered.

'I really think I need one,' she agreed. 'You don't think I'm like a prison wardress, do you?'

'Course I don't,' I said, reaching for the teapot.

Although we were worlds apart in every way, there was something about Patricia I couldn't help liking, a sort of honesty that somehow shone through a brittle exterior. Despite the F/H/B we remained friends and she called, just for a short while, almost daily, always looking stunning in her designer outfits and wearing the obligatory big hat. The F/H/B related to Richard the way he would to a bullied bullock in the field, beating off his tormentor with a big stick.

Patricia would often arrive at Chilcott soon after breakfast to discuss recipes for lunch. She alternated between nouvelle cuisine, decorated with flower petals ('I picked them myself from the garden') covering miniscule grams of coley, to sausages ('I've decided the yellow of marigolds goes particularly well with sausages'). Once, when they were entertaining for lunch she came down to borrow four tomatoes, returning them a few days later with her usual, scrupulous honesty – 'I know you loaned me four tomatoes, but, as you can see, I have brought you back three, as I do think you will find these are slightly larger.'

Her afternoon teas scorned the traditional country fare of scones and cream in favour of cucumber sandwiches with the crusts cut off, which, she explained, was no less than her friends expected.

'What for?' the F/H/B wanted to know.

'Ain't they got no teeth?'

'Of course they've got teeth,' Patricia replied indignantly. 'The Queen always has the crusts cut off her cucumber sandwiches.' The F/H/B scratched his head, striving to piece together the connection between the neighbour's cottage and Buckingham Palace. 'That sort of woman,' he snorted, 'got a job to tell cows' dung from pudding.'

The one certain thing was that there would be plenty of booze to accompany any meal they had with friends. Otherwise, they were said to abstain through the day (although we believed this was not strictly true of Richard) until six o'clock when their serious drinking started. They would both watch the grandfather clock until it chimed six, which galvanised the pair of them into action, when Patricia would have a large whisky and Richard a pink gin – together. Before the half-hour was up she would leave the sitting room, carrying her glass, and refill it from a bottle of whisky hidden in the washing machine. Minutes later Richard would leave the room and head for the garden shed, where he mixed himself another pink gin from his secret hoard. A short while later they would each have an official refill from their starting post at the cocktail cabinet. Then the whole exercise would be repeated. By eight or nine o'clock both would be in their cups, and quarrelsome.

'You're drunk!' she would accuse Richard.

'No, no, my dear, it's you that's drunk,' he would retaliate.

'I can't be – I've only had three...!'

One morning Patricia arrived in the kitchen and sat on the old settle, delicately pleating the hem of her silk skirt. 'I threw the wireless at Richard last night,' she said conversationally.

'It missed him and hit the wall and all the inside fell out on the floor. I picked it up this morning and stuffed it all back in and now it's working perfectly well.' She leaned back against the settle. 'Do you ever think about being a widow?'

'No, never.'

Patricia went on, almost dreamily. 'I've got a friend who wore bright blue to her husband's funeral. I do think she was so brave, don't you? It was a gesture, you know.'

I handed her a cup of tea and changed the subject which was getting a bit out of my depth, vaguely reminding me of an old seaside postcard I had seen on Ilfracombe pier, picturing two fat ladies (they're always fat on seaside postcards) gossiping over a garden wall, with one saying to the other, 'Do you ever think about divorce?' and the other replying, 'No, divorce never, murder, yes.'

◇◇◆◇◇

My Mate Minnie

'Can't you see I'm on my knees kissing a pig?' berated the indignant lady pig keeper when a caller interrupted her tête-à-tête with her porcine friend. Pigs tend to bring out strong feelings in their devoted owners, although Exmoor menfolk claim that both pigs and women could get dangerous if they had a brain. This is an insult of the highest magnitude, particularly to pigs who have an inborn intelligence that defies criticism. Exmoor has never been a pig-breeding area, but the few countrymen who elect to breed a pig or two surprise themselves with the rapport they share with their sows, which transcends black pudding and pork scratchings and moves on to an altogether higher plane of comradeship. They even, so I've heard, have been known to opt out of holidays because "twouldn't be fair to me pigs', and one wife, who for years had dreamed of a holiday in Venezuela was told by her pig-loving husband to pull herself together. 'All you got to do, Maid, is to pick a hot day, stick an infra-red lamp in the pigs' house, git cidered-up and you'm in Venez – whatever you calls it.' It's no wonder that some wives have been heard to complain that their husbands show more respect for their sows, referring to them by their fancy names such as The Baroness whilst the Missus is merely 'Maid'.

Years ago we bought a young gilt from a friend, a whopping pig for her age, already named Minnie. I say 'we', but it was my enterprise as the F/H/B was strictly a sheep man and had no interest in pigs. In the event his lack of interest grew into full-blown antagonism as Minnie pitched her weight at doors, gates and fences. She had an appetite the like of which we had never before encountered, starting on the kitchen garden, which she devastated on her first day's walk-about. Our plan had been to keep her shut in her (we thought) very comfortable pigs' house for a week before letting her out, but Minnie had other ideas, knocking her own little door off its hinges, then repeating the exercise on the main door out into the field. The gate into the kitchen garden presented her no problem at all; she just lifted it off its hinges. Within a week the F/H/B had all but turned the place into a fortress, but still Minnie managed to bulldoze her way through a hedge and visit our neighbour where she consumed a pile of seed potatoes, a brood of eggs due to hatch the next day, and, for good measure, the farmer's trilby hat which was hanging on the gatepost.

Within the next month she visited every farm within walking distance, leaving a trail of destruction. The farm pony had more exercise, as we took it in turns to search for her, than a seaside donkey at bank holiday. After a few such excursions it fell solely to me to trace Minnie and bring her home as she and the F/H/B had a fall-out. Whereas I would carry a few pig-nuts or bits of apple in my pocket and talk quietly to her, encouraging her to follow me home, he took the opposite stance, believing enforced discipline to be the only way to deal with a rebellious pig, swiping at her with his favourite weapon, i.e. his cloth cap, at the same time shouting and swearing, which only served to upset Minnie's sensitivity. He declared that she had turned on him more than once, charging towards him with her jaws open and her fangs showing, which could have been quite frightening, only I refused to believe a word of it. Minnie and I had become close; you could say we were best friends. She followed me, and I never had problems steering her homewards; if there was a hiccup at all it was because she had only two speeds, dead slow and jet-propelled, and she would often pass the pony and me on the run-in. I aimed to keep ahead as her sensitivity was tinged with impatience when she faced a closed gate and with her colossal bulk and strength she could usually manage to shift it, either by sticking her head underneath and lifting it off its hinges, or just using brute force to demolish it.

One afternoon a neighbour phoned, fairly agitated, to say that Minnie was holding them hostage in their own home. The family had just finished tea and were unable to go out to milk their cows as Minnie had taken over their yard and run at them when they tried to cross it, causing them to retreat to the safety of their kitchen, and even there, as they waited, Minnie's face appeared at the open window, thrusting her head through and lifting a bar of soap off the sill. 'Come and get that stinking pig outa here,' they shouted angrily down the phone, 'before one of us shoots it.' There was no time to catch and saddle the pony, so I ran at the double across the fields to the besieged neighbours, confronting Minnie in their yard where she appeared to be aimlessly mooching, blowing soap bubbles from the side of her mouth. She seemed pleased to recognise me and oinck-oinked noisily as I rubbed her hairy ears and we walked home together for once, side by side. I realised then that I loved Minnie. I also realised how enormous, being near enough the size of a donkey, and frightening she must have appeared to outsiders, menacing even, with her open mouth drooling saliva and her little piggy eyes blinking whilst she thought out her next depredation. Then again, looking at it from her angle, it must have been quite upsetting to have missiles hurled at her, as undoubtedly they were, just as she was investigating something new and interesting on somebody else's property.

It was a relief when our large gilt came into season for the first time as we hoped that once she was in the family way she would simmer down and behave like a sensible matron. We booked her in with a boar called William with a good reputation for high productivity, a mere half-dozen miles away. I worried about loading her into our old van, but the F/H/B was confident that, as he put it, any fool can load a pig. Maybe, but not a sow of Minnie's proportions. And Minnie's temperament. The van, later to be christened the pig van, was backed up to the pigs' house, the rear doors opened, and the clean straw inside invitingly sprinkled with a few pig nuts. Minnie sat down on her haunches and stared straight ahead, looking neither to left or right. There was a short ramp to assist her, and a straw bale either side blocking an easy exit. Minnie, for once, was not favouring an easy exit. Minnie was sulking. I felt we needed assistance, and ran indoors to phone Seemingly and another neighbour, the one we called the Pig Expert though to our knowledge he had never kept a pig in his life. The three men put their shoulders to the sow and heaved; I dangled a bucket of pig food from inside the van. Eventually, after what seemed an interminable period of time, brute force won the day, plus the help of a bucket turned over on Minnie's head to block her vision. One more gigantic heave and she was inside the van, doing a smart about-turn to exit the way she had entered, but the back door was already slammed on her and being tied with baler cord. There was a tinkle of glass as her snout appeared through the rear window.

Flushed with success as I climbed into the driver's seat and started the van, I was tempted to celebrate victory with a two-finger Churchillian gesture as I drove past the three sagging shovers who looked all set to spend the rest of the week in intensive care, but I compromised with what probably passed for a satisfied smirk that immediately vanished under a stream of water that gushed over my unprotected head. Minnie, not unnaturally, was a little over-excited.

It was a relief to arrive at William's farm and any trepidation I had over unloading my pig faded as she charged from the van and followed William, who seemed to be expecting her, into his own little cottage, where, the farmer told me, he entertained his visiting ladies. I was disappointed on William's appearance, rather common and loutish for a sow of Minnie's superior breeding.

Minnie stayed away a week and the place didn't seem the same without her. The F/H/B agreed. 'No,' he said, ''tis a bleddy sight better.'

I collected her on the seventh day away and she followed me into the van without demur, oincking and grunting all the way home. I think she was pleased to see me and by way of a welcome home party I slipped her a couple of mangel wurzels I had stolen from the cows' feed. It was easier to steal them than to ask the F/H/B and risk another scene over Minnie's appetite.

It soon became clear that a happy event would be taking place, and, as we had hoped, in view of Minnie's increasing bulk, her forays became limited to her home ground, with just the odd visit to try the feed sheds and an occasional garment off the clothes line.

She eventually produced 14 strapping piglets, a quite extraordinary number for a first litter. She appeared not so much motherly as a general commanding an army. She led the manoeuvres and her small force of commandos backed her up. Everything suffered, but perhaps the garden most of all. The F/H/B used to fairly dance with rage as they all raced delightedly round the daffodil beds, their mouths crammed with our spring display.

At eight weeks of age the piglets were despatched to market and, as we drove in the pig van through Barnstaple, they managed to burst the back doors open and all disappear to mingle with the traffic and crowds. I was sitting in the passenger seat, frozen with dismay, dressed to go shopping and wearing my best high heels, when the F/H/B banged on the side of the van as he chased the piglets, yelling 'Come on, outa it, sat there like a lady, there's pigs out yer!' Luckily, there was plenty of crowd participation, and as we were holding up all the traffic anyway, they were quickly caught and heaved back into the van. I spent the morning shopping in laddered stockings, after just one glimpse at the piglets in their market pens. The sight of their trusting little faces peering out at me made me feel traitorous. They fetched a good price, and once back home I sneaked another mangel wurzel for Minnie and whilst she chomped beside me I marked up a few sums on the door of the pigs' house. What with her rapacious appetite for our own and our neighbour's property, it looked very much like she was still in debt. I gave up. What the heck, I thought, tweaking her ear; you can't put a price on friendship. Anyway, as I stood there I was beginning to dream up a new idea, one that would benefit us all. How about if Minnie had mountains of feed at home, more than she could manage, then surely there would be no need for her to leave home at all? If our neighbours could come up with all their waste, such as old potatoes, unwanted turnips, waste corn, anything edible, she could deal with it at home. It was a scheme that would suit us all and, most important to me, if not to the F/H/B, the sight of our gigantic pig being pursued by purple, perspiring farmers, brandishing cudgels and even shotguns, would be banished from the rural scene. It would give us all peace of mind, a return to tranquillity and friendly relations, and, not only that, maybe next time we marketed piglets they might show a profit. We desperately needed more money, not only to live, but also to support a growing posse of dependants. Apart from Minnie there was the sheepdog and the farm cat, who admittedly both worked for a living but were not directly earning, and a sickly white calf who needed veterinary treatment after being rescued from death's door when a gale demolished its home in a lean-to barn. Then there was a small deformed hen called Gladys who had one eye, the sole survivor out of 50 pullets slaughtered by a fox in one night of savagery. She was so traumatised that she never laid an egg in her life, neither did she stray far from us. Maybe Gladys was not exactly costly to keep, but it all added up on our already tight budget.

I shared my thoughts with Minnie, who blew hard into her mangel wurzel and little pieces skittered in all directions. I thought she looked pleased. My next move was to discuss my idea with the F/H/B. I repeated it to a pair of boots sticking our from under the tractor. He was not impressed. 'I never heard such rubbish in me life,' said the boots. 'Sounds like blackmail to me – a bleddy protection racket, paying up for a pig to stop home. I never heard the like, you'm off yer head, Maid.' The boots waggled indignantly. Minnie and I left them to it and moved on to make our arrangements.

Neighbours were hearteningly co-operative, and several, not all, produced spare feed, the news quickly spreading that consignments would be welcomed in Minnie's little field. It soon piled up with old potatoes, stale bread and buns from the local baker and a surprise dozen or so sacks of infertile eggs from a nearly poultry farm. I could see my basic idea was working, and Minnie never left the place for a single away-day, but it was all swinging out of control, being more than she could handle with a surplus that encouraged extra eaters to take up residence. Vandals in the shape of innumerable cats and dogs and chickens guzzled hungrily throughout the day and fought noisily throughout the night. The second week an unpleasant acrid mist manifested itself over Minnie's larder, with a dominant whiff of addled eggs wafting on the breeze through our kitchen window. In addition I found the chicken farmer had dumped a bag of dead day-old chicks along with the eggs. Things seemed to be taking a runaway course that neither Minnie nor I could handle. I was inclined to agree with the F/H/B when he pointed out, not unreasonably, that we had enough rubbish of our own without collecting everybody else's.

My master plan was veering a bit off course, climaxing one warm, humid morning in Minnie's disappearance from the field. My first thought was that it had all become too much for her sensitivity and she had taken off on one of her excursions, but, mindful of the F/H/B's ruling to 'Always look home first,' I headed for what I thought to be the least likely residence to find Minnie. There she was, stretched out on her own straw bed, pinched and pale with drooping ears, a snivelly snout and a bulging belly. She's dying, I thought, 'She's dying!' I screamed as I ran to fetch the F/H/B, who left his tractor, running at the double, to examine Minnie with all the attention of a practised surgeon. Then he removed his cap, thoughtfully scratched his head, and made his diagnosis. 'She's egg bound,' he said. 'And 'tis all your doing, woman. You stuffed that pig both ends, like stuffing a sausage, and serves the pair of you bleddy right.' And he rammed his cap back on his head and picked his way back through the sloppy jumble outside.

I rubbed Minnie's acre or so of belly and decided to get a second opinion. I called in our neighbour, the self-styled Pig Expert, a fine chap in an emergency. He too arrived at the double, brushing aside the cats and dogs and chickens that had gathered round Minnie, as she remained motionless. Sidestepping a small brown loaf he made his careful examination, and then straightened to give his verdict. 'Her's not quite-hexactly,' he said cautiously. From his poacher's pocket he produced a bottle of physic, and the F/H/B, displeased at all the hassle over a pig, appeared again, obviously hoping to bring the situation to a close, as he cut the toe off an old boot to make a funnel through which they poured the mixture right down Minnie's gullet. She never even blinked, and the F/H/B stood back, looking down on her recumbent mass, and proclaimed, 'Her got two chances, and I ain't too bleddy particular which one 'tis, just so long's I don't hear from you two time-wasters again to day.'

Minnie came up with her first reaction, a deep-seated belch from way down somewhere out of sight. The onlookers scattered, clucking and miaowing, then reassembled a moment later to stare in wonder as she scrambled heavily and awkwardly to her trotters, and set off through the open door out into the sunshine taking little wobbly steps. I nearly cried with relief and turned to thank the menfolk, but the F/H/B was the first to speak. Pointing his finger outside and looking directly at me, he ordered, 'I'll give you just half a day to clear up that stinking mess out there, so get cracking.' I got cracking. As I shovelled and scraped I reflected that in the beginning it had all seemed like a great idea. An intelligent one. But then, the F/H/B always did maintain there's two things a chap should never have doings with, and that's intelligent women and intelligent pigs. A great surge of love for Minnie came over me as I glanced across at her, sunning herself comfortably, her belly down from full-moon size to half-moon size. She was very intelligent, I told myself.

As Minnie grew older and appeared to be more matronly, I fancied she slowed down a bit. She still did very much her own thing and was a familiar figure intermittently roaming the fields and byways. Once she was brought home by the local policeman who found her with a dozen piglets, meandering along the public highway. I thanked him for bringing her home. 'Arresting,' he corrected, sipping his tea.

At least everyone in the area recognised Minnie, which helped, sometimes turning into a sort of spot-the-pig competition, and I would get two or three phone calls for a sighting. One summer's day she was more than a mile away, ambling along the main road holding up a stream of holiday traffic, with sightseers all clicking their cameras at what was quite likely the biggest pig they had ever seen. Luckily we were buddies, and the instant she heard my voice she would turn and follow me. She actively disliked men, and this I attributed to the F/H/B who had absolutely no rapport with her at all; she gave me the impression that she was always striving to get back at him, registering the nearest she could get to a pig laugh right in his face. Men made no impression at all with Minnie, as evidenced one teatime when we heard shouts for help from our yard and Minnie's baritone joining in. We rushed out to find a visiting farmer halfway up a pole, with our sow standing threateningly underneath. He wouldn't descend with Minnie still there, so I shut her in the pigs' house, but the whole scenario had a sort of Keystone Cops flavour to it which even the F/H/B found hilarious. Although he had a great sense of humour, up until then he never seemed to find anything funny to laugh at in pigs, and THAT PIG in particular. We led our neighbour indoors and revived him with a dash of whisky in his tea, while he told us the tale. 'She come right at me, snorting and baring her teeth. I had to go somewhere, so I went up thik pole.' I dismissed it as a poor explanation. 'You should have stood your ground,' I told him. 'She only wanted you to rub her ears. They gets itchy this time of year.'

'So's my backside,' he answered ungraciously. 'But I don't go chasing folk up poles when I wants to scratch.' Which I thought was a singularly impolite answer, particularly from a chapel man who should have set a good example to the rest of us.

Minnie visited her friend William from time to time, and many fine piglets were bred from the relationship, which we sold as eight-week-old weaners. The poorest litter she ever had was of 18, far too many, and with a number of runts. She ended up with ten, which was less than she usually reared, and, because of the large number, undersized and weaker than normal. I could not bear to think that Minnie might be on her way out, or at least heading towards the end of her child-rearing days. She was a good mother; everything she did was to benefit her family. One sweltering day she managed to disjoint our water pipe from our private spring, which left us without a drop of water in the taps, but Minnie and her kids luxuriating in a glorious swimming pool as the water gushed out. I enticed her away as the F/H/B fixed it, but in no time she repeated the exercise, once again draining all our household water from the pipes. There was no stopping her; she repeated the exercise over and over. The piglets loved it, she loved it; the F/H/B went berserk and ended up running an electric fence round the whole area, which stopped her – sometimes.

It was soul-shattering news the day I heard that William had gone for sausages. William had done his duty by Minnie and sired all her piglets. I rushed to tell the F/H/B, but felt so upset I could scarcely get the dreaded words out, 'Williams's gone for sausages!' He was totally unsympathetic and actually said he was glad to hear it, and had I thought about letting 'that old sow' as he called her, join him. I stood my ground and said no, I hadn't, because I expected to find her a new partner without too much hassle.

All the same, this was easier said than done because (a) hardly any farmer in sheep country keeps pigs, and (b) nobody with anywhere half-decent would allow our pig within a gunshot of the place. I commenced my search without any luck until the next market day, when I spotted Charlie, a little wizened gipsy man who lived alone in a shack on a waste piece of ground a couple of miles from us. He kept a few sows and a boar, and he appeared concerned as he respectfully doffed his cap and I explained Minnie's needs, which were then becoming urgent. If I missed her coming into season it meant a delay of another three weeks, and losing time meant losing money. Although Charlie lived quite close, he must never have been on Minnie's visiting list, as there was no glimmer of recognition when I mentioned her name and size. Uncle Charlie, as we all called him, was insistent that I walk Minnie over to him that very evening, and I was glad to agree. The F/H/B sniffed when I told him I had success at last in finding a boar, saying the old chap must be off his head taking in Minnie and next morning would tell the tale of when he woke up to find his shack had gone from round his bed. Minnie and I were happy to set off together into the setting sun, although by the time we arrived it was getting dark as she was in one of her go-slow moods, closely inspecting the buttercups and picking at mouthfuls of sweet, new hedgerow grass. Her new partner was introduced, standing in a thick farmyard crust and with a partially chewed-off ear, looking more than a shade loutish. He was a definite step down the social scale from William who, living in his own little cottage, had actually received visiting ladies in the sitting room.

The old gipsy man made us both welcome and invited me into his shack for a cup of cocoa whilst Lop-ear, as he called him, got acquainted with Minnie.

Once inside kind old Uncle seated me in his best chair whilst he busied himself preparing our cocoa, and I busied myself giving his bachelor shack the once-over. A big notice over the door warned, 'The wicked shall be cast into hell' whilst numerous like observations scattered the walls. My eye wandered from the old gramophone in a corner to a bored looking stuffed owl in a glass case, and on to a brown sepia picture of full-bosomed angels winging their way to heaven. An inscription beneath read sternly 'The end of the world is nigh'. That was as far as I got, as just then Uncle Charlie turned from his gas ring with two steaming pint-mugs of cocoa. Sipping them appreciatively, we chatted about our mutual pig-breeding interests, and by the time I thought about my hazardous journey back home with Minnie, the stars were shining. I was glad to accept Charlie's offer of bed and board for Minnie, together with his suggestion that I collect her the following evening. He even learned over his gate and shouted after me, 'Don't you worry, m'dear, I'll look after her like me own!' If a forty-piece orchestra had struck up a serenade it could not have sounded sweeter than those words of Minnie's new benefactor. I walked – no, marched – off into the night, to gleefully report back to the F/H/B that at last Minnie was top of the pops with one of our neighbours.

The next day, with my heart warming even more to Charlie, I baked him a sizeable sultana cake and carried it with me over to his shack that night. We munched slices with our cocoa, and I listened about the wife who had left because she never understood him, much less his pigs, and I told him I knew just how trying it could be because the F/H/B had no patience at all with my Minnie. We sat together in silent sympathy, and then Charlie suddenly learned across, thrusting his toothless, whiskery face close to mine. 'Give us a kiss,' he demanded. For a few seconds I sat rooted to the best chair, staring at the little forget-me-not text that bade, 'Be though strong and ever faithful.' As though from a great distance I could hear Charlie's voice rambling on that he thought I was a 'proper little woman', and Minnie and me could both stop on for ever. Motivated into action, I dived off the best chair, whizzing past Minnie's benefactor, the stuffed owl in the glass case, the frantic angels and all the flower-garlanded texts and straight out through the door into the twilight.

Fortunately Minnie was lurking near the gate looking as though she, too, had had enough, so the pair of us fled through the gate, my pig being at her jet-propelled best. Racing along neck and neck, I passed Minnie on the home straight and we both swept thankfully into our own yard.

I burst out my story to the F/H/B and before I had finished there was a grunting and squeaking like rusty springs gyrating into motion and the F/H/B commenced laughing, wiping tears from his eyes and saying, 'Well done, Maid – you'll know where to go next time to git that pig seen to for nort!'

Sadly, there was not to be a next time. Minnie farrowed down, but the piglets were not of the size and quality of previous litters, and I realised she had reached the end of her working life. I would have liked her to enjoy retirement ('I never heard such rubbish' was the F/H/B's opinion on the matter), but Minnie, who had caused such controversy in life, settled matters by quietly dying one night soon after she reared her last litter. 'Old bitch,' said the F/H/B almost fondly, as he got out the tractor and digger to bury her. I cried for six weeks. 'Bet you wouldn't do that for me,' he said.

We bought another sow and gradually worked up a little unit of ten sows and a boar, but Minnie was irreplaceable. 'Good job too,' was the F/H/B's unfeeling comment. She certainly left her mark.

◇◇◆◇◇

Summer
Nothin' like a Hound Dog

With the advent of summer my thoughts would turn to chickens, and the necessity of having fresh eggs on hand for visitors' breakfasts. We had long since given up rearing pullets in favour of buying in yearling battery hens, throw-outs, so the poultry keepers would insist, at the end of their productive lives, and, being reasonably plump due to their restricted activity, fit only for boilers. I well remember the first consignment we collected, and all those that ultimately followed from year to year, as behaving initially in such a passive manner as to make me question if they had enough zip left in their flaccid bodies to even repay the £1 a head they had cost me after spending their lives on a poultry conveyor belt. There were 30 of them, and as we carried them from the pig van into the barn, where we laid them on the floor in some straw, they moved not a feather, lying motionless; they could have been dead except for the gleaming of their little dark, boot-button eyes. It took several hours before the little hens struggled to get on to feet that had for the past twelve months been redundant, and three days and some encouragement before they attempted the steps – two of them – through the open barn door and into the yard.

It was anybody's guess as to who derived the most pleasure from this achievement, the hens or myself, as I watched them take in the wonders of the Great Outside, exploring, scratching, creating luxurious dust-baths, and then, ultimately, work. And how they worked; from inside the farmhouse I could hear their happy clucks as they laid their eggs, digging out nests in the hay and straw, often so high up as to be well nigh inaccessible. Howsoever, this was not a problem with summer visitors always willing to seize a bucket and go egg-hunting; it seemed to give them a real feeling of participating in country life, not as hazardous as riding the pony and less energetic than walking miles round the sheep. And, best of all, it was 'getting something for nothing', an illusion shared, by many of the egg-hunters. This was also shared by mushroom gatherers who consider what they like to call 'food for free' should be liberally shared around. I know of one farmer who caught a family in his field filling carrier bags with mushrooms. 'Hey,' he yelled, exasperated, 'they mushrooms is a £1 a pound.'

'Righteo,' yelled back Dad, 'how many do you want?'

When it comes to gathering mushrooms hazards manifest themselves to the uninitiated in the form of other non-edible fungi, often growing alongside the mushrooms. At Chilcott it was not just the children who brought in bags full of toadstools; adults were equally guilty, and if I had cooked all their offerings we would probably be dead by now. It was far better to keep off the subject of field mushrooms and confine the children to the hay and straw barn searching for undiscovered nests of eggs, in fact sometimes they went undiscovered for so long that chicks were hatched.

∘◇◆◇∘

Adults often showed the same enthusiasm as children for rooting around in the barn, but usually for different reasons, with courting couples sneaking a cuddle behind the bales. And not just courting couples, come to that. I can recall what must have been at least one adulterous liaison. This was when Mr and Mrs Grimshire from the Midlands came to stay, together with their son and daughter-in-law. Father was a tall, handsome man who looked like he had crept along at the same snail's pace all his life, and nothing would ever change that. His son, around thirty I thought, took after him except for his wild-professor appearance, with spectacular frizzled hair that gave him a look I can only describe as startled, as though he was plugged into the Mains. His wife, on the other hand, was a complete contrast, a bubbly little blonde with wide china-blue saucer eyes, a real baby doll in tight-fitting blouses that strained at the buttons. The F/H/B and I pondered, over our supper, how she ever came to be involved with her husband, and even he was stumped for an answer, the best he could come up with being 'Must've bin a dark night and her said yes and meaned no.'

The chairperson and director of the whole proceedings was Mother, a fearsome-looking lady with a black moustache which waggled when she talked, which was virtually non-stop, a woman it would not have been unkind to describe as butch. It would have come as no surprise to see her spitting tobacco juice down the front-garden wall and hoisting a shoulder holster. She berated her husband constantly, particularly for some reason best known to herself, at dinnertime, and with an audience present. He never answered back, quietly studying the food on his plate, a broken man, and even managed a sort of enigmatic half smile throughout. He had probably learned over the years to shut out the tirade and never heard a word as he spooned mustard on to his steak and kidney pie. The rest of us heard it though, an incessant rant. 'Look at him sitting there, a useless, spineless slob. I'm the one who earns and he's the one who spends, it's thanks to me we're on holiday. Listen to this, he started work eight o'clock at his last job, he did, got the sack at half-past and got sent home with a day's pay. You know what they said? They said half an hour of him was long enough and if they give'd him a day's pay for nothing they'd be in profit. There, that tells you something, don't it, but I'm the one that's got to put up with him, it's back home to Muggins, that's where he goes.' She paused for breath and waggled her moustache fearsomely whilst her victim, pleasant and smiling, studied a forkful of carrot on its way to his mouth. His calmness served to incense his wife. 'Then there was our wedding anniversary, and what happened? He turns up half an hour late, that's what happens, and not a penny in his pocket, and I got to pay for the pictures and a curry, all on me own because he's gone home in a huff.'

'Listen, my dear,' the F/H/B interjected, finally. 'You don't have to do your dirty washing in this dining room, and besides that your dinner's getting cold. You're s'posed to be here for a happy holiday.'

'I don't do holidays,' replied the butch lady, 'I'm busy, busy, busy. Anybody wants anything done, they ask me. You can ask me, go on, tell me what to do and I'll get up in the morning and show you what's what, nothing ever stops me from work, not holidays, not nothing.'

'Right, then, me dear,' said the F/H/B, never known to refuse an offer from workers. 'Right, you can start tomorrow morning after breakfast cleaning out the cows' muck.'

'Not that sort of job,' remonstrated the new worker. 'That's a dirty old job, I want a nice clean one.'

'Look,' said the F/H/B, 'you asked for a job and I've just give'd you one. Take it or leave it, please yourself.'

'Not shovelling, I don't want shovelling.'

'All right. You can go in the barn and pick up eggs, but you'll have to climb around a bit.'

'That's better,' said Mrs Grimshire, the moustache widening into what was almost a smile.

For the next three or four mornings she zealously picked up the eggs, but then it rained. 'I'm not going across the yard in this sort of weather,' she declared. 'I'd sooner stop in bed and read.' Bunty, the daughter-in-law, quickly stepped in, offering to take her place, and on the way out somehow collected her father-in-law. When they returned they were both flushed and their jumpers were covered in hayseeds and chicken feathers. From the titters of the other guests they were obviously the subject of some speculation. The F/H/B was remarkably restrained, not speaking a single word, just haw-haw-hawing with his shoulders heaving and thwacking his knee repeatedly with his hand. From that day on Mrs Grimshire senior lost her egg-collecting job to Mrs Grimshire junior, who made sure she beat her to the hay shed, getting up earlier every day. Mr Grimshire senior, also, started taking an early-morning walk, because, he said, in one of his rare sentences, it was doing him so much good. His smirk broadened noticeably, his wife affected not to notice the feathers and they hay seeds, and neither did the son, well, not to our knowledge. 'He never will,' said the F/H/B reflectively, 'you only got to look at the stag that begat him to see that.' We never heard from the family for many years, then someone from their area told us that Mrs Grimshire had run off with a bingo caller from their local Pleasure Dome. Of Mr Grimshire there was no news. We wondered if his smile had stretched to a hearty laugh...

◇◇◆◇◇

A popular addition to farm life in the summer were the hound puppies which we reared annually for the Dulverton East Foxhounds, returning them to kennels every autumn when they were nine or ten months old, to be replaced the following spring with new eight-week-old puppies. The purpose of farming them out was a necessary part of their upbringing, getting them used to sheep and farm animals in general, and learning their names, plus a modicum of discipline – that is if such a thing is possible with a hound puppy. Hounds are pack dogs, not to be compared to collies, who are biddable, on a mental high and ever eager to learn. All hounds want to do is hunt, which, after all, is what they are bred for.

Every year Master would hand over to us a shy, whimpering, cuddlesome eight-week-old bundle of puppy, and every year I would think perhaps this one would be different. It never was, of course. It was all of 99 hound puppies ago when it all started with a pathetic looking little animal called Bampton. It must have been the year of the Bs, which signifies to the huntsman the year the puppy was born. Bampton did not stay pathetic for long, and soon developed a circle of friends off his own bat. The first was an unlikely friendship with one of our ginger cats, Mr Slick, his next best friends again unlikely, being Richard and Patricia in the cottage up the road, who encouraged the pair to make their lawn their HQ. The inseparable cat and puppy would disappear every morning to race back and forth on the immaculate lawn, collecting odd souvenirs to play with and leaving some of their own. They eventually inveigled themselves into the cottage where they reclined in luxury which came to an abrupt end when Bampton chewed the leg off an antique table, then, pursued by an irate Richard into the garden, snatched his spectacles off the kitchen table, and raced hither and thither with Mr Slick running behind grabbing at his tail, followed by their victim brandishing the table leg. 'I almost lost my temper,' Richard explained to us later. But still he found the hound puppy, and his constant companion, too irresistible to banish, albeit he tried to keep his doors locked from them. I feverently hoped they would never again gain admission, particularly as Patricia had, on one of her visits to Chilcott, inadvertently knocked a little china horse off a shelf and broken it. Her apologies were profuse as she gazed down at the shattered remains on the flagstones and she finished with, 'But how lucky it happened in your house and not mine – my pieces are mostly Meissen, you know.' I swept up the little horse and told myself you cannot put a price on good neighbours and Patricia and Richard were, all in all, very tolerant of our animals when they invaded their property.

Oddly, they appeared more tolerant towards our animals than our visitors. Although they would often chat to our guests, they never encouraged them inside their house to view their treasures. They became quite friendly with one couple, John and Ruth, who lived in the New Forest, and even proffered them tea on the lawn, but before they left Patricia informed them that she was not going to invite them indoors, although, she ended graciously, 'You may look through the windows.' This became a catchphrase, when John and Ruth telephoned us from their home they were quite likely to commence with, 'We're coming up to look through the windows!'

The next puppy to be landed on us was a little bitch called Basket. If Bampton was a survivor, Basket was a loser, and not the most engaging of puppies, always hung up in a fence, or AWOL, or sneaking off round some corner or other, not altogether a lovable bundle of hound puppy. She matured rapidly to an unbelievable ugliness and had the adventure of her life when a couple of our visitors walked to the beauty spot of Tarr Steps, some five miles distant, and she followed. The couple, a dentist and his wife, from Surrey, were not exactly endearing and I wondered just what they were doing holidaying on Exmoor. They walked a bit, which somehow seemed out of character as they were uninterested in the countryside, and had a very urban outlook on life. The F/H/B and I came to the conclusion that they were either here to (a) get their weight down or (b) on a self-inflicted fitness course which involved walking X number of miles everyday. The F/H/B had his own views on so-called fitness programmes. 'Ask 'em to do a day's work and they'd collapse afore dinner,' was his considered opinion.

I remember it was on a Wednesday when we missed Basket around mid-morning, but as she had then reached about nine months of age, I concluded she had probably gone off on one of her little rabbit hunts. When teatime came and went and there was still no sign of her I started to worry, but it was impossible to commence a search as the visitors' dinnertime was looming and the F/H/B had, unaccountably, taken himself off to bed with what he called a 'touch of the nadgers'. I managed to catch the visitors on their return to ask them if they by any chance had sighted Basket in their travels. Yes they had, said the dentist, but not since that morning when she had followed them to Tarr Steps. But where was she now, I wanted to know.

'No idea,' was the uncaring reply. 'We lost the dog when we got there and haven't seen her since.'

'You mean you just left the dog five miles away and came home without her?' I was aghast at their indifferent attitude.

'Well, there were other dogs there, and children. I expect she's still there playing.' The expression on my face must have said it all as I dashed off to haul the F/H/B from his sickbed, less than pleased, to go and look for Basket.

'Maid, I knowed that couple was useless soon as I seen 'em,' he growled, tugging on his shirt. 'All bleddy airs and graces, I'll give they a piece of my mind, see if I don't.' True to his word, I heard him confront them in the cider room. 'What the hell do you think you been up to, taking that dog away from here,' he wanted to know.

'Oh, we didn't take the dog, it just followed us up the road.'

'You could have soon enough kicked her backside home,' was his rejoinder. It was the turn of the dentist's wife to chime in with, 'We could never have done that, that would be cruel.'

The F/H/B rat-tatted back with, 'And I s'pose what you done ain't cruel, walking off and leaving a dog to stop out all night.'

The couple weren't going down without a parting shot. 'Well, it's a hunting dog anyway, and we don't approve of hunting, as such. Now that is cruel.' They couldn't get away with that, not with the F/H/B. 'Listen,' he said 'you don't approve of us, and I'll tell 'ee something, I don't approve of you. Don't you even bother to come here again; this ain't your sort of country. There's a place for you and that's in Butlin's holiday camp, locked up out the way.' And the F/H/B, looking angry and not very well, stumped off to start the pig wagon to commence the search for Basket. He was some time before he returned, complete with a chastened-looking hound. He recounted that there had been no sign of her along the road, nor at Tarr Steps, which by that time of evening was well-nigh deserted, but after a few enquiries he found that the farmer at Tarr Farm had safely caught and kennelled the hound, thinking that eventually someone would be looking for her. Her ear-tag identified her as belonging to the Dulverton East Foxhounds, but he told the F/H/B, hound puppies that were being walked often gravitated to Tarr Steps where they would rendezvous with their friends and spend the day dashing in and out of the river. If Basket had been fed with holidaymakers' bits and pieces of cake and sandwiches she gave no sign, mopping up her dinner as ravenous as she ever was. I turned to the F/H/B, remembering he was none too well when he left the house. 'Have a whisky and go back to bed,' I advised.

'I ain't going back to no bed,' he replied defiantly.

'But I thought you said you had 'flu earlier on.'

'And so I did, Maid, but that been and gone – I'll have the whisky, though, just the same. Medicinal, that's what 'tis.'

After her big adventure, Basket, to our surprise, did not seem disposed to join again the games at Tarr Steps. In fact, strangely enough for a hound of her age, she spent her time sitting in the yard, howling ceaselessly. Before long, unbelievably in one so young, her increasing girth proclaimed that she had, indeed, something to howl about. I blamed the F/H/B for not manning the barricades and allowing all her escapades. He blamed me for over-feeding ('It makes 'em saxy'). Seemingly turned up to referee and pass his opinion, for what it was worth, just staring at the rotund bitch and pronouncing, 'Her ain't quite hexackly.' On Boxing Day she produced eight identical puppies. Identical, that is to our sheepdog, old Skipper.

Shamed and disgraced that we had failed so miserably to take proper care of our hound, we played safe for a few years, insisting on dog hounds only. Of these Why Not was my all-time favourite. He was a lovable idiot and my problems with him stemmed mostly from his improbable name. One morning I heard a sales rep in the yard calling enquiringly 'Yoo-hoo.' From an upstairs window I noticed the hound pounce playfully on him as he repeated his 'Yoo-hoo.' I poked my head out the window and shouted 'Why Not.' The rep looked faintly surprised and explained he was looking for the farmer, but perhaps I could help. 'Why Not!' I screeched as I noticed the hound pawing at the man's immaculate suit. The salesman persevered. 'We are offering some new lines in worm drenches and udder cream and I wonder if you would like to sample them…?'

'Why Not,' I yelled at the misbehaving hound, shaking my mop threateningly out of the window. 'Perhaps I'll call back later,' conceded the rep, heading for his car. It was only as he drove away that I realised he must have still been scratching his head over his one-sided conversation with a woman whose vocabulary comprised of two words, repeated over and over.

Much the same happened with some ramblers that the puppy attached himself to as they walked past the yard. They banged on the back door and said they had brought him back as he was following them up the road and they did not want to encourage him to stray. 'Why Not,' I said, looking down at him, smiling and wagging his tail.

'Well, you wouldn't want to lose him, would you?' said in the conciliatory tone used for a four-year-old.

'Why Not,' I said, bending to pat his head, and then, turning to the ramblers, I told them, 'this puppy needs watching twenty-four hours a day, he's off here, there and everywhere.' From the looks on their faces I realised they must have thought I was trying to get rid of him, which led me to hastily explain that his name was Why Not. Over the months that he lived with us I became very attached to him, and he to me, although he seemed to love everybody and showed his affection in his haste to greet callers by taking short cuts across the dung heap, bearing small gifts in his mouth, which he dropped at their feet. Old bones, dead mice and even the mummified remains of a rat were all unearthed as presents for his friends. One Sunday afternoon Why Not was racing around the lawn disturbing visitors who had spread out their car rug to lie down on for a peaceful snooze. Ignoring him seemed to work, as he went away, but duly returned at the double, carrying a small skeleton in his month and landing with a thud in the middle of their colourful tartan rug. The visitors had had enough by then and with swift presence of mind they jumped up and, deftly gathering up the four corners of the rug, attempted to carry Why Not to the stable to lock him in. There was a rending of cloth as the hound's four legs went straight through the rug, followed by his substantial body, still holding his gift in his mouth. Luckily the visitors thought the whole episode hilarious and dined out on it for years after.

There can only be one thing more distracting than one hound puppy, and that is – you've guessed it – two hound puppies. I was surprised to see our normally gentlemanly Master across the Square in Dulverton one day, waggling two fingers in my direction. All was explained the following day when he turned up with not one, as expected, but two hound puppies.

'Never,' we both cried together, and, 'sorry, Master, definitely not,' but somehow, after Master left, there we were glaring at one another over two of the little dears and chorusing, ''Tis all your

fault – you give'd way.' They were brother and sister and, ultimately, turned into a fearsome combination, Factor the dog, being
all brawn and no brain, and Fairy the bitch, being thinking. The
F/H/B flatly refused to call the bitch Fairy ('If you think I'm going
across they fields shouting Fairy with all the neighbours listening
in and laughing, then you got another thing coming!'). So,
somehow, she never properly learnt her name and they both
thought they were called Factor. They investigated everywhere,
thoroughly, and particularly any campers. They would leave their
straw beds in the stable and move into tents with the smallest
encouragement, and campers in our fields reported back frequently
that both puppies would be stretched out on their beds or even
inside their sleeping bags. One dyspeptic camper had his indigestion pills stolen and swallowed by Factor, and the puppies seemed
to build up a cache of stolen goods. Watching them, there was no
doubt that Fairy was the brains behind the outfit and Factor was
the hit man, gormless but carrying more weight than the little bitch.
They stole a child's purse containing £2.70, holiday money, which
was mercifully intact, and together they raided the Scouts'
weekend camp and returned carrying the Union Flag between
them, half each, which they must have compromised on, as by then
it was in tatters. We returned the remains and the dutiful Scouts
hauled the rags up their flagpole and saluted them. Sightings were
also reported of Fairy and Factor further afield, in East Anstey
churchyard, to be precise, where they raced round the gravestones
unravelling a piece of knitting they had stolen from persons
unknown. (It certainly was not mine, as I would sooner, you've
guessed it, pluck a pheasant than struggle with plain and purl.)

The puppies grew into fine hounds and the F/H/B enjoyed his
usual love/hate relationship with them, blaming them for every little
disaster that happened during their childhood with us. I remember
one windy autumn night when we were asleep in bed and a slate
crashed off the roof above us, and the F/H/B tossed in his sleep and
muttered, 'I'll kill they bleddy hound puppies for that!' But, try as he
would to incriminate them, he had to concede the next morning that
it was unlikely that even Factor and Fairy had climbed on to the roof
at dead of night and slung off a few slates just for the hell of it. They
lived in their own apartment, a small unused stable assigned to

hound puppies, which by the time they left to commence their training in the kennels was barricaded like Fort Knox in the hope of keeping the residents at home. The farm dog, old Skipper at that time, would sit tolerantly watching the hounds going about their depredations, as much as to say, 'If I'd behaved like that at their age I'd be run out of town by now.' Generally, the resident animals suffered the puppies' arrivals and departures as part of their seasonal cycle as with visitors' dogs, seemingly aware that they were just short-stay comers at Chilcott. When the hounds departed they left a gap always, but none more so than Fairy and Factor, particularly with the neighbours. They loved visiting and once managed to bulldoze their way into a garage which was housing goods for a forthcoming jumble sale. Unseen, they must have made countless journeys back and forth to Cow Field, which was their favourite playground, carrying various items including top-to-toe ladies' wear and one high-heeled fashion shoe that looked, when we found it, more suitable to Piccadilly Circus than Cow Field. Amongst the goodies was a straw hat and an alarm clock which had stopped at twelve o'clock, and the F/H/B said, 'Right, Maid, that's the time to-day they two's going back to kennels – I've had enough,' and, true to his word, he bundled them in the pig wagon and set off. I felt sad, knowing they were leaving their childhood behind them. We had plenty of reminders of them when we shovelled out Fort Knox, in the shape of bones, turnips, a half-knitted sock still on knitting needles, another Piccadilly Circus shoe, the remains of a nightdress and a grey vase with R.I.P. imprinted on it. I felt a lump in my throat looking at their treasured belongings, but I knew I would be seeing them again, if not before, then at the puppy show the next July, when I would lead them into the show ring with the other couples to be judged for prizes. By then they would be eighteen months old, but of course they all recognised their puppy walkers.

The puppy show at the kennels is a great occasion, the Big Event of the summer for most of us, an occasion set up by the Masters for puppy walkers and farmers whose land the hunt travels over, and any subscribers who are specially invited. The kennels are the huntsman's pride and are always presented to the visiting public newly painted and whitewashed, surrounded by neatly mown lawns and colourful hanging baskets. The hounds are catalogued in leaflets, and then called in to a little show ring to be paraded in pairs before the visiting judges, usually Masters or ex-Masters or huntsmen from other packs. Once the prizewinners are selected, dogs, bitches, and couples, we all roar off to the village hall to partake of a sumptuous tea generously provided by the Masters, followed by the awards for the winning hounds, with a silver teaspoon presented for every hound walked. Of the 33 teaspoons I have collected over the past years only once did I win a Best Hound award, and that was with Fairy, she of the rampageous Fairy/Factor combination. I was as taken aback as the F/H/B as we both considered Factor to be the superior hound in both looks and conformation, but the judges obviously concluded otherwise. At the tea excitement got the better of me and I was hard pressed to manage a single jam and cream cutround. The prizes were to be presented by no less a personality than His Grace the Duke of Beaufort, and commenced with the Best Dog Hound which went without a hitch, the Duke charming and smiling as he presented the prize and shook the hand of the successful puppy-walker. Me next, I thought, and my stomach churned, not helped by the realisation, too late, that somehow I had drifted to the back and would have to walk the length of the hall to collect my prize. The Master, who may or may not have, had a tincture or two by then, read the citation, which came out as 'First-prize bitch, Mrs Huxtable.' A great roar of delighted laughter greeted this statement followed by raucous cheers as I picked my way through the hall for what should have been my moment of glory. It felt like running the gauntlet; the normally urbane (it was not his first visit) Duke could not contain his merriment and the F/H/B was hysterical for the rest of the day and most of the night. The prize I collected was a silver platter, which serves to remind me to this day of a special occasion in more ways than one, together with two silver teaspoons engraved with the names Fairy and Factor. All the spoons are slotted into carved wooden holders which now hang in the dining room at Chilcott and when I wield the Brasso I have an instant roll-call of names recorded in my memory as permanently as on the spoons themselves. Recollections crowd in as I go from Adamant, who was a tough, good-looking sort, to Dalesman who was trouble free and kept his nose clean throughout his puppyhood. Dabchick was a little, pale bitch who never looked quite strong enough to withstand the hoo-roosh of joining the pack, then there were Swiftly and Swallow, Whalebone and Whittle (of the same era as Why Not), and Gratitude (a misnomer if ever there was one) and all the others who followed on after Fairy and Falcon. There was also, sadly, one puppy who never made it to the presentation, having been run over by a car up on the top road, unseen and unreported, a sad sign of the times we live in when hounds are discounted or even deliberately driven at by a certain section who represent themselves as animal lovers and are deeply opposed to hunting, citing it as cruel. Nature is cruel in many ways, but it is natural, whereas driving deliberately over a dog is an appalling act of savagery and bigotry that I hope never to witness a second time. The first, and only, time I witnessed such a distressing act was when the huntsman of the Dulverton East Foxhounds was bringing hounds through the main road into Dulverton and the driver of a maroon-coloured car suddenly accelerated, driving straight at a hound that had strayed a few yards from the main pack. The hound was thrown in the air on impact, then lay crumpled in the road, dying, until passers by, momentarily traumatised by the malevolence of the attack, dragged it, yelping in pain, into the gutter and the huntsman despatched it with his humane killer. Such was the turmoil that no one thought to take the number of the killer's car, which quickly accelerated away out of sight. It was a sad end to our day, and a sad reflection on a society wreaking revenge on an animal simply to emphasise their own fanatical point of view.

A hound may be only one dog in a pack, but to the huntsman they are all individuals as are our own dogs, and it is sad and distressing to lose an animal, either by death or disappearance. Terriers have been known to vanish down badger sets or even rabbit burrows, and never resurface, their frantic owners mustering an army of diggers in the hope – often in vain – of finding them still alive. So it was one cold November when we sighted an old collie dog wandering around the nearby lanes and fields, aimless and obviously lost. The F/H/B attempted to encourage him into the stables in an effort to catch him, believing his owner would certainly be scouring the countryside, ever hopeful of tracking him down, but the old collie was timid, running off to a safe distance then standing at bay, staring, like an old stag. I thought he might be sniffing around for a bitch, but the F/H/B was scornful, saying that from the look of him that would have been wishful thinking. I reported him to the police station in Dulverton, but was told there were no missing dogs listed, but they did take notes of his description should there be any enquiries. He was sighted by various neighbours for all of six weeks, then, one cold, rainy morning Seemingly looked in to report that the old dog was dead in one of our fields and he was looking for a shovel to dig a grave. I felt sorrowful, for although we had tried, off and on, to catch him, I felt we should have tried harder. The F/H/B collected a couple of shovels and went out with Seemingly to lend a hand with the sad task, but in no time at all they were back in the kitchen, the F/H/B jeeringly laughing at our neighbour as he scoffed, 'Call yourself a stockman when you can't tell if something is living or dead!' I gathered from the conversation that when they arrived in the field to conduct the funeral, the corpse stood up on his old, wobbly legs, had a good shake, and lolloped off to a safe distance. The old collie, they said, was sleeping rough; he was thin, undernourished, and obviously stone deaf. We decided we must all put out food for him and use it to entice him into captivity where at least he would have a warm bed and we could step up the search for his owner. Several more days passed and the food disappeared every night, but whether the dog or some other predator was eating it was impossible to tell. Eventually Richard and Patricia phoned jubilant that they had enticed the old collie into a shed and slammed the door on him. Could I take him away they asked, so I set off with an old collar and a piece of baler cord, opening their shed door cautiously, fearing the old dog might object to being cornered. He looked at me warily, but he had a wonderfully kind old face, and, although cowering, allowed me to hitch the collar and baler cord round his neck, and I half-dragged him, somewhat mistrustful, from the shed down to an empty stable in our yard. I fed him with dog biscuits and a tin of meat and he seemed grateful, looking up at me as he crunched his way through every morsel, finally licking his lips and giving a faint wave of his tail. Later that night I again slipped the baler cord through the old collar I had given him, and walked him up the lane, and this set a pattern for the following weeks, every night and morning.

The next day we stood him outside in the yard and closed the gate, although he looked too decrepit to make a run for it. Seemingly joined us for an inspection, remarking that nobody could be missing him from work, as he must have been pensioned off some years past. He had a long sable-coloured coat, but it was matted like an old piece of knitting that had been left out in the rain. His tail was the best bit of him, curling over his back like a great ostrich plume. His white front was muddied and covered a worryingly wheezy chest. His legs were shaky and his feet flat and splayed. He was painfully thin and covered in fleas and he was stone deaf. 'Fourteen if he's a day,' said the F/H/B and Seemingly nodded agreement, ruffling the fur covering the skinny frame of what once must have been a very good-looking dog. ''Tis only the fleas what's holding him together,' he observed, peering into the shaggy coat.

'Right then, Maid,' the F/H/B instructed. 'You'd bestway ring our P.C. again and say we caught the old stray and for God's sake get somebody to collect him afore he pegs out.' The policeman repeated that no dog had been reported missing, and he could only suggest the animal might have been dumped on the moor. This was so shocking and so unheard of in the countryside that as I rushed to tell the menfolk who were still in the yard gossiping over the old dog's head, tears started to trickle down my cheeks and they looked at me aghast as I mopped my face on my sleeve. 'Now what?' demanded the F/H/B. 'Cough it up, Maid, what's go wrong?' I pointed at the cause of it all, who by then had decided to take the weight, such as it was, off his old legs, and was stretched out on a small patch of grass. With an effort I repeated the policeman's words and both the men were incredulous that someone, from somewhere else, could have deliberately landed an old dog in such a cruel predicament. Our neighbour clearly thought it a possibility, rocking on his naily-booted heels and nodding, 'Seemingly so, seemingly so,' whilst the F/H/B took matters in hand, with a practical, 'Now then, Maid, us won't give up yet awhile, us'll keep'n a couple more weeks, you can stick a advert in the paper, you never know, somebody might turn up. Now for cripes' sake turn off they bleddy waterworks and fetch us out buckets and brishes.'

Seemingly filled the buckets from the water trough and the F/H/B threw in a measure of sheep dip to oust the flea infestation in the old dog's coat. I held him, with a piece of baler cord wound round his jaws as a muzzle, but he seemed unconcerned at all the brushing and combing, which reinforced our growing theory that he had been more of a pet than a working dog. After his scouring we left him sitting outside to dry off, but kept the yard gate closed as a precaution. I went indoors to phone a few neighbours in what now seemed to be an increasingly unlikely event that one of them might have heard of a lost dog. I missed out on our singing farmers as I knew they were both working in their fields, having heard snatches of 'Baby it's cold outside' drifting up the valley as they duetted in full loving blast. Not one of our neighbours was able to help, although they all showed concern and promised enquiries of their own. That week I bought up all the local papers and looked up the Lost & Found columns, all to no avail until the following Friday, and suddenly, there he was in the *West Somerset Free Press*, a full-blown photograph smiling at us from the back page with – LOST–BEN – inscribed above it in dark capitals, together with a telephone number for Watchet, some twenty-odd miles away. So that was his name, I thought, as I dialled the Watchet number, yes, he looked like a Ben, a good old much-loved retainer. A woman, who sounded a dead ringer for our neighbour Patricia, answered and I excitedly rat-tatted out the good news that her dog was safe at Chilcott. To say I was surprised at her reaction was an understatement. 'Just describe him to me,' she said, diffident to the point of coolness. I described the old dog, together with all his afflictions. No, she told me, he was certainly not deaf.

'Possibly,' I ventured, 'he had a knock from a car on his travels, a bang on his head that affected his hearing?' The lady snorted as delicately as her up-market voice allowed.

'Highly unlikely, I would say.'

But, I protested, he was very old.

'No, he's only eight and in his prime.'

What about his wheezy chest, was he asthmatic?

'Certainly not. No, not ever.'

I felt as though I were floundering. I knew I had the dog matching the photograph; there was no mistaking it. I tried an invitation. 'Would you like to come over and see the dog? You'd be very welcome and it would set all our minds at rest.'

'No,' said the cool voice. 'I've got Mother staying and it would be a wasted journey. He's clearly nothing to do with us, I'm afraid I can't help you,' and click, the phone went dead.

I recounted my astonishing conversation to the F/H/B when he came in to tea and together we pondered over the mystery of it all; after all, why bother to advertise if you don't want your dog back, and maybe he'd had some sort of accident in his travels which made him appear more decrepit than his age. Nevertheless, any frantic owner would have motored not just from Watchet but hundreds of miles to check for themselves whether it was their dog or not. We again poured over the photograph, slightly blurred but a distinct likeness.

''Tis he right enough,' said the F/H/B. 'What the hell be 'em playing at? I tell you what, Maid, I'll bet a thousand pounds to a penny nobody else wants the poor old bugger. Now hand me another piece of that yeast cake and next time you make one put more currants in – looks like they been fired in from a gunshot away.'

Two weeks later the old dog was still with us, still eating voraciously, but reinvented. His legs were less wobbly, he walked on his flat feet with as near to a spring in his step as he was ever likely to get, his wheezy chest had stopped playing a tune, the sheep-dip had done its stuff with the fleas, and, above all, he had become trusting and looking happier. We still walked out together twice a day but there was no need for us to be attached by baler cord, he stayed as close as he could get, looking up at me and wagging his tail. We had bonded. Happily for him his life had turned about; he had a full belly, a comfortable straw bed and new friends in the shape of Skipper our sheepdog, and the farm cats who liked to sit purring beside him. None of them seemed put off in that there was still a distinct whiff of sheep-dip hanging over him. His feed dish was always emptied, but I found out that any leftovers were carefully removed and buried in a hidey-hole, his safeguard against ever starving again. He was not to know that a new threat was looming, as the F/H/B remembered his ultimatum of about keeping the old dog for a couple of weeks.

'Right, Maid,' he said, as the two of us returned from our morning walk, 'get him down to the vet and have him put down. No point in keeping him here at his age.'

'I can't, I can't,' I cried. 'He's my buddy now, I love the old chap.'

'Listen,' countered the F/H/B, 'I told you he's all of fourteen, he can't be going to live a lot longer, anyways. Now be off with you.' It was time to make a stand. 'Please, oh, please,' I pleaded. 'Can't I just keep him – tell you what I'll have him for my Christmas present. I don't want anything else, honest, just to keep the old dog – and if he's not going to live long it won't matter much, will it?'

The F/H/B, whose bark was worse than his bite, capitulated incredibly quickly, which made me think he was glad to relent.

'Waste of bleddy time,' he grumbled. 'But's that it, and I don't want to hear another word, and don't you forget neither, that's your Christmas present attended to, and that's final.' As he turned to stump off he patted the old dog in passing. I was so overjoyed I flung my arms round my new buddy and kissed him on the top of his head, then, for good measure, I chased after my husband and kissed him, too. He looked a bit taken aback and wiped his mouth with the back of his hand. 'You taste of sheep dip,' was all he said.

The news soon spread that the old stray had taken up permanent residence at Chilcott, and such was the interest generated that he started to receive visitors in his own right. Richard and Patricia arrived, carrying a bag of dog biscuits. 'You mustn't over indulge him, you know,' said Patricia, as I opened the bag and fed him one.

'Why not?' asked the F/H/B. 'You overindulge every bleddy night of the year.'

'I am not going to lower myself to answer that,' she replied icily.

'No, because you know 'tis true,' goaded her tormentor as I hastily intervened by offering tea all round.

Even George and Nellie showed up, actually on another matter, but had a look at the dog whilst there. Nellie's comment was brief as she jabbed her thumb-stick in his direction. 'You want to kick 'ees ass homewards,' she advised. 'You be mazed as a brish taking that old thing in. More money than sense, that's what I sez. Betterfit you gived me some of it.' George stood and smiled at the recipient of his wife's wrath who waved his tail and smiled back as Nellie said, 'You can wipe that smirk off your face and start to think about doing some work for a change.' This was presumably to George, although her look encompassed them both. She emphasised it with another wave of her thumb-stick as they both set off up the road for home. They never ever came in for tea, nor did they ever entertain. They both carried little hip flasks concealed in pockets somewhere out of sight, the contents a secret to all but themselves, as they were never offered around. Speculation ran high that it was a secret kick-arse concoction invented by Nellie, top-strength for her and watered down for George. Nobody ever found out.

As the old dog settled into his new life at Chilcott I found the greatest difficulty was not being able to communicate. His hearing had totally gone, so I decided I would try to teach him some sign language by just waggling my fingers at him. Come here, sit, wait, all simple signs, but he was bright, with focused eyes, and it was successful. We became inseparable; too inseparable because when some of our guests offered to take him on a walk it proved impossible. I slotted baler cord through his collar, but they never got out of the yard, such was the fuss he made. He sat down and howled as though being beaten by a stick, and when they attempted to walk on they had to drag him behind. They got no further than the gate, such was his distress; it was like he thought he was being dragged from home to be abandoned again. They gave up and he fell over his own old legs in his urgency to get back to what had become his perch on the kitchen doorstep. I noted that he never once crossed the threshold to come inside the house, an indication that he was accustomed to living outside, which smacked more of a working dog than a pet. All we had on him were conflicting theories.

Whilst being wary of strangers to the extent of refusing to leave the yard with them, he would struggle to his feet and follow me everywhere, clinging, as the F/H/B put it, closer than the ivy to the old garden wall. One spring day we set off to sow corn in our farthest field with the old dog lolloping along following the tractor and drill, which was not worrying at first. The F/H/B drove the tractor and I rode the corn drill, keeping it topped up with seeds and shoving it in and out of gear on the corners. The dog could see me and started off to try and keep up with us on every round, panting, with his eyes rolling and his tongue hanging out and getting ever more exhausted. I stepped off the drill and sat him down by the gate and waggled my fingers at him with the 'stay' signals I had boasted to the F/H/B he had learnt and understood, but as soon as I climbed back on the drill and we took off across the field he was right behind, nearing a seizure with every effort. Finally, after another round, the F/H/B stopped the tractor and ordered me to take the old dog home, which meant a delay of at least fifteen minutes, and did not please a working farmer. As I left the field I closed my ears to the barrage of abuse that followed us, though I did make out something like '...and make sure you lock'n up, he's a bleddy liability and you encourage 'n!' I made sure, but realised that for the next few weeks he was likely to be persona non grata; the F/H/B was not a man to forgive and forget.

Amazingly, the old dog was soon to inveigle himself back into favour with a job he created for himself. He became a minder. It started with a tiny orphan lamb I was warming in the oven of the Rayburn. It recovered enough to roll out of the oven, struggle to its feet and totter to the back door, which was open to the spring sunshine. It fell off the top step onto the dog who was stretched out on the bottom step. He seemed unperturbed, merely sniffing curiously at the unexpected landing of a small, strange animal, which seemed to have dropped from the sky. He gave it a tentative lick and the lamb snuggled into the cosiness of the old dog's fur, the beginning of a friendship which led to them spending their days together and, eventually, their nights. I would feed the lamb from a bottle with a teat on it four times a day, and the old dog caught all the drips.

He eventually reared a whole succession of orphan lambs, watching benignly over his charges, like a loving old grandfather, which led to us finally naming him Granddad, mainly for reference. As the F/H/B once said we could have called him Mr Hitler and he would not have been any the wiser. After that first lamb our annual allocation of two hound puppies arrived, to be speedily introduced to their minder, and from the very first night they moved into his stable, where, we guessed, they all three slept soundly as there was not a single whimper for their mother. This set a pattern with the puppies going to bed with their new Granddad every night and getting up with him in the morning, and during the day he would often venture up the road with his charges to visit the neighbours. Richard and Patricia were 'charmed' as she expressed it and wanted all the friends they had made to meet the trio. Patricia's invitations usually followed the same pattern, starting with, 'Do you think Granddad and the puppies could come up at teatime today, I've some rather important people coming and I know they would love to see them.' The

F/H/B queried this statement once with, 'Tell me, Patricia, what hexactly do you mean by "important"?' accompanied by his steady stare designed to unnerve her.

'Why,' she answered staring back, 'of course they are important. I must say these are not quite intellectuals, but they are definitely semi-intellectuals.'

The F/H/B leaned across the kitchen table, interested. 'You mean half-wits?' he asked.

'No, no, no, a semi-intellectual is not a half-wit...' she was floundering. 'Well,' she finished cuttingly, 'it is so stimulating to meet people with whom one can have an intelligent conversation – not that it isn't awfully nice living in the countryside, but one does tend to miss 'er conversations.'

'Even with half-wits?' concluded the F/H/B.

''Er yes no. Don't confuse me, Arthur.'

'It doesn't take a lot,' he said cuttingly.

Nevertheless, I was always grateful to Richard and Patricia for being so good with the dogs and even encouraging them to play on their beautifully kept lawn. Whatever depredations they wreaked, they never complained or banned them.

Granddad's reputation as a minder spread and once, when he was taking a few days' respite from his nursery job, a neighbour turned up with two tiny terrier pups for him to look after whilst their mother visited the vet. He readily accepted them with the same good nature he extended to all our own animals. Then, when our little ginger cat had kittens he minded them, allowing them to play with his ears and his bushy tail whilst their mother went on a mousing expedition. She brought the kittens back a tiny dead fieldmouse to play with, whilst Granddad looked on indulgently.

One summer a TV film crew turned up from the 'About Britain' series to make a film centred on Chilcott to be called 'The Farmer's Wife', and there was Granddad, captured for ever on the video I now have, with his tail waving, waiting to greet the hound puppies as the Master delivered them. It was then we found out that filming is all about events being moulded, or even distorted, in some cases, to fit in with the film makers' schedule. In other words, a fix. The hound puppies arrival did not fit in with the film makers' scheme of things, and as they came from Bristol everything had to revolve around their arrangements. By the time they were ready the puppies had, in fact, already been in residence at Chilcott for over a week. The director, a practical, charming chap told us, 'Well, we'll just have to cheat a little bit.' Words we were to hear over and over during their five days of filming. Cheating meant that the Master was directed to turn up for a second time, load the pups into his Land Rover and drive up the road, turn round and come back for the pups to 'arrive', with me running down the yard yelling excitedly, 'The hound puppies have come!' a sequence which I stumbled over at least ten times. 'You've run past the cameras – you're too quick, too slow, we couldn't hear…' Try as I would I could not get it right and I felt the director was trying hard to be patient. 'I'm not an actress,' I told him once.

'Thank gawd for that!' was his uninspiring reply. He was helpful, finding an old piece of bone and placing it where I was to start my shout. 'Start to yell when you get to the bone,' he instructed patiently. This was soon followed with, 'That's no good, you were looking for the bone!' and then, 'Didn't you see it? You were too late again!' Eventually it came right and the director, if not entirely satisfied, made the best of a bad job and we moved on to the Master's arrival with the puppies, a charade performed especially for the cameras which went well owing mainly to Mr Burton's faultless delivery in his Warwickshire accent.

Filming ground to a halt once more when Patricia arrived in the yard sauntering before the cameras, her tall figure elegant in moleskin trousers and a canary yellow polo-necked sweater. It was a hot day and I wondered why the sweater, but all was to be revealed in the following days of filming when her interest in fashion decreed she should never appear at any event dressed inappropriately. When the harvest was being filmed Patricia sashayed on to the scene clad in a backless sun top and tiny shorts obviously cut down that morning from a pair of slacks, revealing her lily-white, stick thin legs at which the F/H/B pointedly closed his eyes and turned away. Her grand finale was at the puppy show in which she appeared in all her sophisticated glory in a screen-printed silk two-piece topped off with a head-turning floppy straw hat covered in tea roses that was so sensational it made the film. Richard kept well out of focus.

The film crew numbered around ten, with Daniel Farson a local interviewer providing the continuity, and each night prior to filming the following day, the director would ring asking that I bake steak and kidney pie for dinner to be followed by bread and butter pudding and cream. They would clear every morsel. One of the crew was a very attractive blonde who was obviously madly in love with one of the cameramen and they went into a clinch every time there was a check. The director would hustle them back to their jobs with a bellow of 'Coitus Interruptus time again!', and feel sure he thought we had no idea of what he was referring to, but we had been taking visitors for a long time and our education owed a lot to them.

The F/H/B steadfastly refused to be interviewed on film until the last day, which was to climax with a picnic at Exford Horse Show. The director insisted that he said a few words, if only to show his presence, otherwise it looked as though I lived alone. The guests that were staying that week came with us and I spent half the night before cooking for the picnic for about 20 people in all. The setting was between Winsford Hill and Exford, with a background of wonderful scenery that almost looked like a stage setting, and teeming all around with beautifully groomed show horses and ponies. But the F/H/B's interview would hardly have won him an Oscar and could not have been exactly what the director had in mind.

'Do you have any favourite guests?'

'Oh, aye.'

'So are you sorry when they leave?'

'Yeah, course I am, but I gives 'em a bag of pig-shit for their garden.' This gem ended up on the cutting-room floor, alongside me falling under the horse's belly when the saddle slipped. We were shown all these out-takes when the film was finally edited and we were invited to Bristol for lunch with the director. He evidently thought it the right time for some plain speaking to the F/H/B. 'I know what you're been thinking about me,' he commenced.

'Too bleddy true,' came the answer.

'Well, I'm not you know, I'm not that way inclined. I've got a wife and a couple of kids at home.'

'You coulda fooled me,' said the F/H/B, unrepentant.

Granddad made it through the film but died suddenly soon after, sleeping away one night in his own bed in the stable. I was distraught and everybody who had ever met him mourned the old dog. He had lived with us for nearly five years and died owing us nothing, so willingly had be worked with his small charges, and so freely given his love. He had obviously been nowhere near as old as we first thought which again added credence to the newspaper advertisement for the eight-year-old Ben from Watchet. We wondered if his owner who so scathingly dismissed his return would see the film and recognise him. Their loss was our gain.

After the film was shown on TV we were inundated for three days with phone calls, many of them people appealing for a free farm holiday. One was a parson who said he and his wife had spent their lives looking after other people and he thought it was about time somebody did something for them. 'We would like to come to your farm for a couple of weeks,' he told me. 'No not now, it's too cold shall we say when the weather is better, June or July.'

'Scrounging old bugger,' was the F/H/B's verdict on that one. He was more magnanimous over the lady who rang to say she liked the look of the ginger cats.

'I would like just one,' she said, 'and perhaps you'll be good enough to deliver it to me in Cornwall.'

'Tell her she can have the lot,' said the F/H/B, 'and I'll chuck in a bag of tetties along with 'em.' I attempted to freeze my generous man with a single look after telling the cat-lady I would never part with any of the gingers. She kept trying, coming back at me with, 'Don't you think that's being rather selfish? After all, you have five and I don't even have one!'

'Goodbye,' I said, hanging up. Others phoned just to say how much they had enjoyed a country programme, and there was one man who thought he recognised my voice from the radio, and I answered the phone to hear him saying, ''Scuse me, Missus, but be you Minnie the pig?'

'Yes!' I shouted joyfully, realising that at some stage he must have listened to Minnie's exploits on 'Woman's Hour', and was a fan of hers. I had to tell him she had since gone to the Great Piggery in the sky.

The summers at Chilcott came and went and we had plenty of good weeks for us to renew old friendships with returning guests. To be a landlady you need a strong compulsion to look after other people, to feed them great food and give them great holidays, but even then we sometimes had empty rooms, which we were glad to fill. Times have now moved on, with more people moving to Exmoor to start up what they are pleased to call 'a dear little B & B' and empty rooms no longer exist. They have metamorphosed into 'availability'. Call it what you like, these casual visitors are invaluable when you're counting heads on pillows.

One such couple were Mr and Mrs Gilbert who turned up unexpectedly looking for accommodation, together with their three-year-old son and a white poodle. I offered them the four-poster room with a single bed in one corner, and they booked in for five nights. They peered into the sitting room and Mr Gilbert dismissed it after one airy glance, saying, 'No different from ours at home, 'cept ours is bigger and got more beams.' He had little passion, he told us, for old houses, and every spare minute he had was spent shooting. He had, in fact, brought his gun on holiday and hoped for a bit of rough shooting, so the F/H/B pointed him in the direction of our wood. His wife scarcely spoke other than to ask for an ashtray from which she was never parted, dogging her husband's footsteps with her fag in one hand and the ashtray in the other. Her silence was more than balanced by her husband's non-stop torrent of words, passably imitated by their small son, Jeffrey.

'He's hyper,' said Mummy, momentarily breaking her silence and taking a deep drag on her cigarette. 'Our dog's better behaved than he is.'

I agreed. I felt I could live with their poodle far better than their child. Mr Gilbert struck me as being highly volatile and it sounded as though the boy turned after him. The family retired to bed early that night and the F/H/B forecast, 'What's the betting Missus and the kid are in the double bed and Father's in the single.' The next day I was able gleefully to tell him he was wrong. When I took their morning tea in at eight o'clock I found Mrs Gilbert and Jeffrey crowded in the single bed in the corner, and her husband and the poodle in the four-poster. Over breakfast Mr Gilbert was quivering with excitement over the thought of going off shooting, and disappeared down to our little wood before the others had even left the table. The F/H/B reckoned he must have fired off 70 shots with his 12-bore, and never hit a thing. Each morning followed the same pattern without as much as a rabbit or a pigeon for the pot. Not that it seemed to worry him, even when one of the lady guests told him she felt she dare not take a walk within a mile of the place, especially if she was wearing her hat with a feather in it.

'No need for you to worry,' he told her. 'Experts know how to handle firearms, and if you're firing a double barrel…' and he was off on what we soon recognised as his two favourite subjects, namely himself and shooting. We never found out what he did for a living as he dismissed the F/H/B's probes with a hearty laugh and his explanation of, 'A bit of this and a bit of that', and his wife busied herself stubbing out her fag into the ashtray in her other hand. 'Bleddy bloke's a mystery,' was the F/H/B's verdict. My advice to him was to leave well alone; more holidaymakers than not aim to leave their work at home and just relax, whilst others, in particular bachelors, live their work morning, noon and night, expounding knowledge generally on subjects most of us are ignorant of and would prefer to stay that way. Only the month before there had been a little man with us who worked on maintenance in Leeds Corporation bus depot, and who recounted in mechanics jargon the state of the buses and the repairs necessary for safety and how the driver of the No. 9 had refused to take it out because the windscreen had not been properly cleaned. It seemed now that Mr Gilbert might well be running a parallel with his gun-speak, particularly as the other guests that week showed no more interest in firearms than the previous ones had shown in Leeds Corporation bus depot.

Following the initial morning shoot-out in the wood Mr and Mrs Gilbert and Jeffrey piled into their car, with the wife driving and father and son together in the back. The poodle, Snowy, was left in her basket in their bedroom with instructions for 'someone' (I was the only one there) to let her outside twice, and to make sure dog and basket, hopefully united, were dragged across the floor in an anti-clockwise direction as the sun moved round. This, presumably, was because Snowy was permanently shivering and needed all the warmth she could get. Looking after the poodle was not a problem, I was just thankful they never left their monster child behind. Little Jeffrey had already had a near-miss with our sheepdog who, like us, was not over child-friendly, and a confrontation with our diesel tank, turning on the tap and covering himself in diesel and spilling enough fuel to run the tractor for a week. The F/H/B remarked that if Mummy had had a fag on the go then it could have been curtains for all of us.

Over the next few days reports started filtering in from neighbours that there was a car being driven round Exmoor with a madman in the back firing a gun through the window. The F/H/B had no doubt in his mind that it was our trigger-happy guest, whom he had already renamed Wild Bill Hickock. Shooting from windows is not entirely unknown on Exmoor; a farmer friend of ours in Taunton hospital instructed his wife to take in his gun so that he could shoot from his sickbed at a rabbit on the lawn (she refused, and three days later she was worried that he had gone into a decline when in fact he was still sulking).

The F/H/B applauded what he considered to be a sporting gesture from a gallant gentleman, but he was less impressed with Wild Bill Hickock's random shooting from a moving vehicle, confronting him one afternoon as he came into the house carrying his shotgun. He told him that taking a loaded gun in a car is an offence and not only that, Exmoor folk were nervous for their livestock. 'Tell 'em they'll just have to get tin hats for 'em,' was the jaunty reply, whilst Wild Bill junior pointed a toy gun at the F/H/B and shouted, 'Bang – Bang, you're dead!' I thought the F/H/B was remarkably restrained, although I sensed they were hardly in the running for the Best Guests of the Year Prize, an award made annually with the first-prize winner collecting a bag of pig muck and a week in our caravan in January, whilst the second prizewinner gained not only the pig muck but a fortnight in the caravan in January. Wild Bill and his wife planned to leave on the Friday as early as 6am for their drive back to Birmingham, and Mrs Gilbert broke her silence to tell me not to get up for them, as they would help themselves to cornflakes and toast, a little kindness that I much appreciated. That night at dinner the conversation centred round the departed family. 'I felt sorry for her,' imparted one of the ladies. 'She really loved it here, said she was dreading going back to their council house, condemned, it was, too.'

Poor Mrs Gilbert, though she didn't have a lot going for her other than her chain-smoking; I could only hope she remained healthy. Wild Bill junior had the last laugh however; he had climbed on the tractor and switched on the ignition. But not off…

◇◇◆◇◇

Kill or Cure

It was inevitable, I suppose, that over the years a certain number of health problems occurred amongst the guests. One lady was perturbed that she could not be given a special injection from a doctor as it was bank holiday, but as she had brought the necessary injection with her the F/H/B volunteered to administer it.

'Are you sure?' she asked doubtfully. 'I mean, have you ever done this sort of thing before?'

'All the time, Missus,' he reassured her. ''Tis just that 'tis pigs and sheep I attends to, can't see no difference meself. Done a sheep I have just this mornin'.' From the trouser pocket of his corduroys he withdrew a hypodermic syringe with the sharp end imbedded in a cork. 'There you be, m'dear,' he said waving the evidence of his veterinary skill before his likely patient. 'My Missus can boil this 'un up in a saucepan if you'm worried you'll git maggots. If not, let's have your stuff, then bend over!'

'It is not like that at all,' said the would-be patient a trifle coldly. 'I'll have my own syringe together with the serum and it is always injected into my leg, not – not – where you seem to be suggesting.'

'Please yourself, m'dear,' said the F/H/B replacing the hypodermic in his pocket. 'Only if you'd just make your mind up, I got to get on. If you just say the word I'll do it and I guarantee you won't feel a thing.'

'How do you know that?' asked the lady, still dubious.

'Well, I never had anybody complain yet!' chortled the F/H/B, thwacking his knee with his hand in his merriment.

The upshot of it was the operation took place in the privacy of the lady's bedroom, and they obviously bonded there and then from the amount of giggling that went on. I heard the F/H/B say, 'Right m'dear, shall I go higher down or lower up?' and the giggles turned into peals of hilarity. I thought it only right that I should keep out of the way.

The F/H/B was at his best dealing with illness, which was just as well as medication for humans was never my strong suit. Some of the guests who arrived inevitably brought their ailments with them, some developed an illness whilst on holiday and other unfortunates had accidents, including umpteen children who fell in the trout pond, though none of them managed to drown, and most of them seemed to regard it as some sort of achievement over their schoolmates. Of the more serious complaints there were two dog bites, one perforated ulcer and several bruisings after falling from the pony, though only one ended up having hospital treatment. There was a broken leg, brought about by the F/H/B at harvest time heaving a bale of hay with such force that it connected with a lady helper's leg on the first day of her holiday, one child with a clipped ear, who the F/H/B caught throwing stones at the chickens, one toothless gentleman whose dentures were washed out of his mouth by a big wave at Saunton Sands, and a second toothless gent who lost his teeth down a lavatory at the Carnarvon Arms. I personally retrieved the latter, which highlighted my unstinting devotion to my guests (or so I kept reminding them) as I am revolted by both sick (the cause of the calamity), and false teeth (I was frightened by a top set as a child). There was also a happy ending for the man who lost his dentures in the sea as he was told by the beach attendant to return the next day as there was a possibility that they could be washed up at high tide, as indeed they were. In fact, our guest reported, he was cheered to find he was not alone in his predicament as there, neatly arranged on a small shelf in the beach attendant's hut, were five sets of bizarrely grinning teeth. 'They'll all be claimed back by tonight,' said the affable beachcomber, holding out his hand.

Although most accidents with teeth bring about raucous hilarity from both the F/H/B and myself, paradoxically I can never forget the horror that two of our guests, both Northcountry gentlemen, suffered when they fell victims to heart attacks whilst on holiday at Chilcott. Amazingly, they both occurred in the same place (Dulverton car park) in the same circumstances (over-heated cars), in the same month (July), but in different years. The first one was, together with his wife, one of our guests of many years from Blackpool; he recovered well enough after a spell in hospital to graduate to bed-rest at Chilcott, where, he said, every night in his bedroom he felt like a ship's captain on the bridge listening to the drunken crew down below partying. After a couple of weeks he was told by the local doctor he could go home, but must on no account drive himself, which resulted in the F/H/B driving him and his wife to Blackpool and returning by train the next day. Before his return he was shown around Blackpool on a whistle-stop tour, which, he said, was a revelation, it being the start of Wakes Week. He reckoned he had never seen so much sick or so much lettered rock in what he then realised was his sheltered life in the West Country.

The second heart attack victim, John West was a new guest who had only stayed with us for a couple of days. His wife rang from Dulverton to tell me he had been taken to hospital, and asking to be picked up as their car was broken down. The F/H/B was not at home, having taken the car to his brother's farm in North Devon, leaving me the old pig wagon, which was loaded with half a ton of animal feedstuff, and not travelling very well, to boot. I drove down, feedstuff and all, to pick up Mrs West and had scarcely arrived back and made her tea when the hospital rang to say Mr West was 'rather poorly' as they put it, and could I get his wife there as quickly as possible. Oh, God, I thought, he's dying, and I mustn't tell her, and I'll never get to Taunton with all that load of feed in the back. I raced out to the yard, opened the back doors of the van, and dragged the feed-bags into the nearest shed. It took for ever. I composed my red and sweaty face into what I hoped passed for a more serene look, and found Mrs West had finished her tea in the cool of the sitting room. My heart was thudding as I told myself she must never know he's dying, and I said as casually as possible, 'Shall we pop to Taunton and see John – I can run over in the pig van, if you like.'

'Oh I would, I would,' she answered gratefully. 'But have you got time? I mean it's nearly thirty miles, isn't it?'

'No problem,' I said, sweating. The pig van hiccupped up the road like it was on its last legs and I fought more rising panic as I viewed the petrol gauge which rested permanently on E. It was too risky not to fill up so I pulled into the local garage, urging the owner to speed up the refill as I explained in whispers my predicament. His response was immediate. 'Take my car,' he ordered. 'You've got a problem and we're here to help – go on, keys are in it.' It was a godsend; the car was so fast after the pig van it felt like we were flying. We arrived at the hospital in what seemed like a record for that particular journey, to find Mr West slightly better, but his wife elected to stay the night. I drove back to the garage and switched vehicles again and arrived home to find a state of panic. The F/H/B had arrived back and found my note on the kitchen table, which, written in haste, simply read, 'Gone to hospital.' Had there been an accident, was I bleeding to death, or found I was suffering from some frightening leurgy? He was so happy to see me that I was reminded of his Auntie who woke up in hospital after falling through her greenhouse to find Uncle planting a kiss on her cheek, which distressed her almost to the point of relapse. 'I knew I must be dying,' she said afterwards. 'He hadn't done that for years!'

Mr West recovered enough to eventually return home to Yorkshire, and luckily his wife was able to drive the car but, sadly, his number was up and he died six months later from an unrelated illness.

Farms are not always the safe places promoted in holiday brochures. 'Come and milk a cow' they offer, which is fine until the cow tires of endless inexpert tugging on her titties, spreads her legs, lifts her tail and has a good clear out over an unsuspecting head. A pony can lift a leg and get one in where it hurts most, and even a mild-mannered sheep can turn into an over-protective virago when she has a lamb, and charges, head down, right behind human knees, with the force of a pile-driver. These foreseeable accidents are there, waiting to happen, not just to visitors but also in the everyday life of any farmer. It is the unforeseeable one that causes the problems, like the innocuous piled-up fleeces in the shearing shed, which the F/H/B fell off, hitting the stone floor with a resounding thud. Afterwards he complained of aching ribs, but soldiered on for a further three weeks, trying to avoid both coughing and laughing, to ease the pain. Our guests were aware of this and toned down their conversations in respect of the situation until one morning when Billy, a bookie from Essex, turned up in the kitchen as we were just finishing breakfast. He had a great sense of humour, but looked serious, as he wanted to recount a tale concerning his wife. 'It's not funny,' he reassured the F/H/B, 'so you won't hurt yourself laughing.'

'That's all right, me boy,' was the answer. 'If you've got a problem it can help to tell somebody. You talk and us'll listen.' The F/H/B was sitting on the old backless kitchen form on the outside of the table, and he pointed Billy to the old settle next to me.'

'You see,' he commenced, 'there's this chap chasing my Missus, and one day I corner him up and I sez, "Come on, then, let's hear what sort of woman you fancy, like," and he looks at me a bit like he's up a monkey tree, so I sez, "How about a woman with big squashy lips that whistles through her teeth like an old buzzard? Fancy that do ya?"

"No, I don't," he sez. "Then how about a woman with big boobies that go flop from north to south when she's starkers?"

"No, I can't do with that," he sez, right on. "Well," I sez going in for the kill, "How do you fancy one with a big backside hoisted like a stallion till she takes her stays off, then 'tis look-out, run for cover," and he looks like he's gonna be sick right down his smartarse Pringle jumper, and he sez a bit faint-like, "Cripes, no, never!" and I say, loud and clear, "Well then, stop away from my Missus!"'

Then, turning to the F/H/B he finished, 'There, I told you 'twas nothing to laugh about, just a bit sad, really.'

The effect of this story on the F/H/B was instantaneous, a bit like lighting the blue touch paper to a rocket as he exploded with laughter and agony simultaneously, firing himself off the form on to the flagstones, lying there gasping, 'Oh, me ribs, me ribs, now I've broke 'em,' then turning to the comedian who was the cause of it all, 'You silly bugger, Billy, 'tis all your fault – oh, ah, oh – get the doctor, Maid, I ain't stopping down here all day, I got work to do, and then us got the puppy show...'

And, indeed, it was our most looked forward to and glorious day of the summer, the showing of our hound puppies that we had walked, followed by a lavish tea in the village hall.

Before the doctor arrived the guests all filed past the patient as he lay on the floor, his head propped on a red velvet cushion that one of them fetched from the sitting room. They talked amongst themselves as though he could either not hear or not comprehend. 'Your dada went just like that,' said a mother to her daughter.

'My hubby did, too,' said another lady, 'with us one minute and gawn the next.'

'It's only his ribs,' I reminded them, but if they heard they heeded not. They stepped over him, they looked down on him, and one lady burst into tears. 'He's always been a good man,' she lamented. 'It only ever happens to the best. He'll never be forgotten!'

'For God's sake shut up,' ordered the patient, coming to life. 'You'm making me laugh again and oh, oh, oh, cripes, I can't stick it, it hurts like hell.'

More speculation was halted by the arrival of the doctor who, without doubt, would be in the front row of the puppy show that day. He wasted no time on sympathy, commencing by laughing uproariously, then spluttering, 'Well, Arthur, old boy, there's one place you won't be going today, and you know as well as I do where that is!' He tried, unsuccessfully, to contain his merriment. 'Never mind, if I can manage your tea as well as my own I'll do that for you – all those cream cakes, absolutely splendid, eh, what!'

'Get me up on me feet, doctor, then sod off,' said Arthur ungratefully.

I attended the puppy show without the F/H/B that year, but he was not home alone, Billy felt it was the least he could do to keep him company. 'I admit I feel responsible,' he said in answer to the wrath piled on him from the other guests. 'So, all right, I broke the no-laughing pact.' Then, with an air of injured innocence, 'I can't help it, can I, if I want to confide my personal problems to Arthur – I mean, I'm living it, it's not funny to me...' No one was taken in by his tongue-in-cheek attitude, but the F/H/B was never one to bear a grudge, not if there was a laugh in it. He just wished Billy had picked a less important day.

As sound travels faster than light on Exmoor, news of an accident at Chilcott brought in the neighbours, all proffering expert advice to the patient. The two sisters, Auntie Julie and Auntie Dolly, arrived wearing their best brown boots bearing some of their special, secret- recipe yeast cake, already sliced and thickly buttered, to which they knew the F/H/B to be partial. 'Eat plenty of fat,' they instructed, 'and make sure you drink a small glassful of cod liver oil every day, topped up with a spoonful of black treacle. Good for all your system.'

Seemingly turned up with a bottle of sloe gin left over from the previous winter, and offered similar advice in the area of lubrication, but with a more alcoholic slant.

Richard and Patricia arrived carrying a floral arrangement and a bottle wrapped tightly in fancy paper with a blue rosette tied artistically round the neck. Patricia told us she had just collected her floral arrangement from the local show, and was not too surprised at not winning a prize. 'I know exactly why,' she said plummily. 'My arrangement is so avant garde for this area, the judges don't mark for style, rustic is more the order of the day.' She gave a tinkling laugh, and I quickly said how pretty the flowers looked before the F/H/B got his mouth open to expound some rustic observations. The kitchen seemed to be filling up with visitors and sloe gin was proving so popular a lubricant, it was running low. The timing was about right to start on the bottle that Richard and Patricia had brought, so I handed it to the F/H/B to unwrap. I noticed Auntie Dolly and Auntie Julie had drained their glasses in anticipation of another beverage and another round but their eyes glazed as an unfamiliar bottle emerged from its wrapping. It was as solidly British as the sloe gin, but sloe gin it was not; neither was it whisky, wine or bubbly. The label read simply LUCOZADE. The F/H/B broke the silence, leaning as far forward as his ribs would allow, towards Richard and Patricia.

'Thank you very much, m'dears,' he said. 'Am I supposed to drink it or rub it in?'

'It gives you energy,' explained Patricia.

'What do he want with energy?' Seemingly wanted to know. 'He's just sat there doing nort, morning, noon and night!'

'Pass your glasses,' said the F/H/B, closing one eye in the direction of the Aunties as he unscrewed the stopper. 'Might git rid of the worms if nort else!' I was not so sure that the contents of that particular bottle would be appreciated, so I hurried to the dairy to collect a bottle of Grouse. It was worth it, just to see their eyes light up as I set it on the kitchen table.

That night, hardly daring to move in bed lest I connected with the cracked ribs next to me, I lay there thinking that cowboys riding the range could hardly come tougher than West Country folk. Nevertheless, at the first twinge of what they call the 'nadgers' or the 'Leurgy' they scuttle to review the contents of their medicine cupboard, mainly because they fear delay might precipitate a visit to the doctor's surgery, or the vet's practice, easily the more popular of the two. Our medicine cupboard reveals cough mixture for horses, worm drenches for cats, dogs, pigs and sheep, udder cream for cows with sore titties, and sprays for inside ears, down throats and under tails. There's castor oil to make 'em go and kaolin to stop 'em, and a tin of black treacle that works wonders in reaching hidden parts. As far as I could remember the human medicines were restricted to a pack of corn plasters and, unaccountably, an old bottle of gravy browning, whilst one single bottle of cattle drench, labelled All-in-One, cancelled out the lot. This is the business; serious stuff for real men, that once uncorked sees the rise of faint blue smoke curling into the air. It is kill or cure, and unlikely to be acclaimed by either vets or doctors. They all agree you've got two chances; you either end up dead or revitalised, I knew that if the F/H/B thought it would have done any good, then he would have had a swig from it, and not for the first time. As I lay sleepless in bed, staring at the ceiling in the moonlight, I recalled the time he was in bed with what seemed to be 'flu and Seemingly called in to sick visit. He looked at my ailing farmer and unhesitatingly prescribed a dose of All-in-One and we turned out the medicine cupboard until we found an old, dust-covered bottle of that magic elixir right at the back. We studied the faded directions and worked out a measure between a large sheep and a small bullock, pouring it into a small glass and topping it up with whisky, to make it palatable. Seemingly propped the patient up on his pillows, saying, 'Right, squire, down this in one and 'twon't touch yer sides.' It worried me that the F/H/B looked peaky and decidedly unwell, and obviously felt it, because he did exactly as Seemingly instructed, without even sniffing it. The potion might not have touched his sides, but it stimulated something somewhere, way down out of sight, his face flamed and he let out a bellow that would have done justice to a first-time calver. 'Me guts,' he gasped, 'me guts is afire!' He collapsed on to the pillows and Seemingly looked well pleased, satisfied that the All-in-One drench had commenced its healing work. We went down to the kitchen and he picked up the bottle that I had left on the kitchen table and patted it.

'Kill or cure,' he said. 'Poured a full bottle once down a heifer that was off her legs.' I was impressed. 'How long did it take for her to stand up?' I wanted to know. 'Well, 'er...' Seemingly hesitated, 'well, Missus, her lived for a couple of days after...'

'You mean... are you telling me she died?'

'No, not right away. You know how 'tis, some you wins, some you loses, 'tis a bit powerful, thik old stuff, specs 'er would have died any ways.'

I suddenly felt faint, but Seemingly was reassuring. 'Now don't you worry, Missus, he'll be all right,' he said, jerking his thumb at the ceiling. 'Us didn't give'n enough to cover a partridge, and even if he ain't cured 'twon't do no harm like.'

I dished up a couple of platefuls of cold beef and pickles for our dinner, and our neighbour went up to check on the patient, reporting back with, 'Sleeping like a babe, seemingly.'

That afternoon, as we were letting the cows back in the shippon, there was a clatter of cats miaowing, chickens clucking, pigs grunting, and a yelping dog, and, wobbling towards us on little, unsteady legs, was the cause of it all, the F/H/B. He turned towards Seemingly muttering quietly to himself, 'Seemingly so, seemingly so, squire.'

'Whatever you gived me,' said the F/H/B, 'was worth a guinea a drop. I feels a new chap – revitalised, you might say.' I fervently wished All-in-One could have had the same effect on cracked ribs. Applied externally, I mused it would probably have much the same result as a rub-down with Jeyes Fluid, with the remedy being more agonising than the complaint. Something like when I was a child with toothache, and my granny would wrap brown paper round my face soaked with vinegar, mustard, pepper and salt. Jeyes Fluid would have seemed refined after that torture.

○◇◆◇○

Autumn
The Bolton Gigolo

Autumn is a time when, hopefully, farmers themselves can take a holiday, but – and there is a very big but – if Missus ever mentions the word holiday our Exmoor man can disappear faster than a rat up a drainpipe. Countrymen just do not rate holidays; they are comfortable working the land they know and love. They don't want strange beds with terminal mattress sag; or shops, wine bars, discos, anywhere without livestock, and, that ultimate horror, beaches. Most countrymen, bulldozed by wife and family into visiting a beach will sit there in his suit with clip-on braces and the *Western Morning News* spread across his head muttering, 'How soon can us go home?'

Holidaying on another farm can be almost acceptable, as it can turn into more of a working vacation. Once, when the F/H/B and I had a two-day break in the New Forest he visited the farm next to where we stayed and castrated all their piglets, then spent the rest of the day riding on their cabbage planter. He also enjoyed a men-only visit to Scotland, their mini-bus party comprising three farmers, two builders, two publicans and a rat catcher, from which the holiday-makers returned looking a shade paler than when they left, hinting of a tour round the distilleries.

Howsoever, failing a short break away it is more than likely we womenfolk will settle for just a day out. When farmers sense this looming they tend to get in first with, 'Right, Maid, us'll have a day up Taunton market.' Not Exeter. Exeter is considered to be a bit smart, sophisticated even, and, as one overruled neighbour put it, only useful for two things – one's to have a haircut and the other's to get drunk. Point-to-points meet with more approval, as do farm sales and a day's hunting.

For those of us whose geography does not extend beyond Blackmoor Gate in North Devon, travelling is often regarded as an expensive luxury. The F/H/B is not alone in pontificating that a week's holiday spent at home resting in bed would work out a sight cheaper, saving on petrol, electricity and food (you don't get so hungry). Whilst a honeymoon might be considered the one obligatory holiday in a lifetime, even then our menfolk can be evasive.

The F/H/B and I did manage our honeymoon together, spending a whole week in Bournemouth, but thereafter the order of the day reverted to separate holidays; it just seemed easier that way with one of us always home on the farm. Come November, after a busy year, I often craved the sun, and one year I teamed up with Mrs Morgan, a little widow who often stayed with us, and we planned to go to Spain, leaving the F/H/B with 14 home-made, plated frozen dinners.

'All you got to do,' I told him, is to reheat one every day in the oven.' He looked unhappy.

'I hate cooking,' he said. As de-freezing one meal a day seemed as much as he could cope with, I left tins of meat and soup to fill the gaps. I knew all about the hazards of freezing soup from my sister-in-law who went away leaving frozen blocks of soup for her husband to de-freeze in a microwave. He never managed to master the mechanics of the miracle heater, telling her afterwards that although the soup was heated it came out in the same solid block as it went in and he ate it with a knife and fork. If I had not hardened my heart I could never have left the F/H/B, he cut such a disconsolate attitude. Nevertheless, I was spurred on by the dream of a relaxing sunshine holiday; I felt I desperately needed it after months of being incarcerated indoors and missing out on what had been a fairly good summer.

With only a week to go before we left, Mrs Morgan, who lived in Lancashire, phoned to ask if she could bring along another lady, Mrs Sidebottom, who was the widow of a vicar. She hardly knew her, but she seemed jolly enough and could be good company. They had found out there was a seat available on the plane, and the apartment we were renting in Calpe, on the Costa Blanca, seemed spacious enough, with two twin-bedded bedrooms. We were all flying to Alicante, myself from Heathrow, and the other two from Manchester, and we had managed to dovetail our flights to arrive within fifteen minutes of one another. My flight arrived spot on, at 6.45pm and the flight from Manchester at 4am. Mine was a scheduled flight, theirs was charter from a firm just about to go bankrupt, or so they discovered when they eventually found their return flight non-existent. I waited and dozed fitfully until the ladies arrived at 4am, and eventually a taxi landed us at the apartment for our sun, sea and sand holiday. We loaded all our luggage in the lift and zoomed up to our penthouse flat on the ninth floor. It was indeed roomy, with a feature fireplace in the living area and bookshelves filled with maps and books in English. Also in English were the numerous notes pinned to the walls, mainly about being sure to water the geraniums on the balcony, not to take the towels on the beach, or leave the taps running at night.

The next morning Mrs Sidebottom was the first to get up, and we soon found out the reason. She had festooned the bathroom with bottles and potions, and one wall was all but covered by a whacking great square holdall split into 48 different compartments, each containing a medication to deal with any evil that might be lurking in a foreign country. Mrs Sidebottom gave us a quick run-through; there were pills for indigestion, diarrhoea, constipation, Beechams pills, mosquito-bite pill if we were bitten, pills to ward them off if we were not, tranquillisers, pills to send us to sleep at night, pills to wake us up in the morning, pills for runny noses, sore throats, hot flushes, cold sweats... the list went on and on. She was inordinately proud of her medications, and at breakfast time (there was a basket of basic food and milk left for us) she arranged rows of coloured pills like soldiers beside her plate, and sprinkled seeds of some sort over everything she ate. After breakfast she produced a bottle of TCP and wiped down every surface in sight. She sprayed her throat two or three times, and offered to do ours. Mrs Morgan and I relaxed on the balcony on the wrought-iron chairs and decided we had made a great choice in the resort. The views were down on to the main street, but it was pleasant and there were glorious flowers everywhere. Behind us, we could hear Mrs Sidebottom hard at work, scrubbing and cleaning the (to us) spotless apartment. She didn't seem to mind, and even popped her head round the door to the balcony to say, 'You just sit there, my little chickens, and leave it all to me. You never know what you might pick up in these foreign places, that's what I always say,' and with a flourish of the scrubbing brush she was back inside tackling the tiled floors.

It was a very breezy day so we opted to go for a walk instead of going on the beach, after all, there would be plenty of days for swimming. We eventually settled for a coffee at a pavement café where we got into conversation with two English ex-pats sitting at the next table. They told us they had just come from church where they had been praying for rain; in fact the whole of Spain had been united in a National Day of Prayer for rain after suffering a drought for the past eight months. That night it started to rain. It also thundered and lightened, the wind howled and the storm thwacked over the wrought-iron balcony furniture and it boomeranged all night, from one end to the other, whilst hailstones the size of marbles bounded down the feature fireplace and across the living room. The lights went out, but one of the notes directed us to candles and matches in a drawer. The water went, and so did the lift. The National Day of Prayer set the pattern for the next two weeks.

The following morning we straightened the overturned table and chairs on the balcony and gazed down at where the street had been to find it replaced with a raging river of muddy water, with cars, bicycles and manhole covers floating down the hill. We put on our beach sandals to go out and buy great containers of water and some more candles and carried everything up 146 stairs to our penthouse apartment. The temperature dropped and we found a single hot-water bottle, which we took turns to share. From our window we watched whole walls being washed away, along with even more cars. There was Calor gas in the apartment, which meant we could heat water and cook, but most evenings we were glad to get out to the one little bodega that was open. Other than that there was nothing to do, nowhere to go; Calpe was just a sunshine resort. With all that rain it reminded me of Ilfracombe in November, but when I phoned the F/H/B he told me the weather at home was glorious, the best November for years.

'Don't know what you lot want to go abroad for when there's this sort of weather home,' he grumbled. 'What's it like with you?'

'Oh, er, changeable,' I told him.

'Aw, so you'm all right, then, Maid. Only I heard somebody say there's torrents of rain somewhere out your way. Lucky it ain't you, that's all.'

'Yes,' I said in a little voice as I hung up; pulling my one jumper I had brought tighter around me. It was cold, and I wore that jumper all day and in bed all night. Mrs Sidebottom, apart from TCP and cleaning materials, had brought several bottles of Sanatogen Tonic Wine in her luggage, and whereas Mrs Morgan and myself spurned her pills and potions, we found the wine, recommended to 'fortify the over-forties', quite acceptable. We decided we might take an outing one day, and found Calpe had a railway station with trains running to Benidorm and beyond. The station was a fair distance from the town and we were rain-drenched by the time we bought our tickets to Benidorm. We believed the train came from Valencia and it was obvious when we boarded that the passengers had embarked some distance away. They were immaculate, and I do mean immaculate. The one that I remember best was a handsome olive-skinned Spanish lady dressed in a beautiful crocheted white suit, with dark stockings and three-inch high-heeled black shoes. Her dark hair was beautifully coiffed and gold jewellery set the whole outfit off to perfection. The three of us were drenched and our flattened hair hung down our necks in lank despair. We managed to find three seats together, but we had scarcely settled down than a little guard appeared, and, from his indications, insisted that we were too wet to sit on the upholstery and would have to stand up for the rest of the journey. Our humiliation was complete when a ripple of laughter erupted from the other bandbox passengers.

We must have been nearing Benidorm when the train stopped outside the station; we gathered there was a landslide on the line and we would have to disembark. The little guard was pacing up and down the track, a good distance below our level, and when he got to our exit he beckoned us down, holding out his arm as though he might catch us if we jumped. Mrs Morgan jumped from our great elevation, straight onto the little guard, knocking him over and falling on top of him. He lost his hat, she lost a shoe, and the passengers all cheered as the two rolled together on the track. Nobody was hurt physically, the shoe was recovered and the guard's hat replaced on his head. We scrubbed Mrs Morgan down as best we could and walked the rest of the way into Benidorm. In spite of all that has been written about it, I have a soft spot for that place to this very day, mainly, I think, because we found a very large tea-room with a live orchestra playing and, at last, we were both dry and warm. Mrs Sidebottom wouldn't let us touch china or cutlery until she had swabbed them with her TCP kitchen paper that she always carried in her handbag, and made a point of doing, ostentatiously.

There was a bar in the café, and Mrs Morgan and I became aware that our companion was smiling and waving at a man standing at the bar. 'Dorothy, who are you waving to?' asked Mrs Morgan, suspiciously.

'That young man,' replied Mrs Sidebottom, 'comes from Bolton, he does.' Mrs Morgan was disbelieving.

'How do you know that? I'd have said with his looks he's Spanish.'

'No, no, lovey, he comes from Bolton. They always wave in Bolton. Very friendly they are.'

'Listen,' said Mrs Morgan, 'I'll bet a thousand pounds to a penny he's not from Bolton. He's Spanish and he's coming this way now and he thinks he's going to get a free drink out of us.'

'Oh, no, lovey, they're not like that from Bolton.' She gave a beaming smile as the young Spaniard pulled out the fourth chair at our table and sat down, at the same time beckoning the waiter.

Mrs Sidebottom learned over. 'What part of Bolton do you come from?' she asked friendly and smiling. He took her hand and kissed it and said something low and sensual in Spanish. She turned to me.

'He's having me on,' she said, 'trying to pretend he's Spanish. Great sense of fun they got in Bolton.' She beamed at him, 'Come on then, tell us where you live.' He ran his fingers up her arm, and I heard the word 'whisky' as the waiter, who had undoubtedly seen it all before, hovered.

'Right,' said Mrs Morgan decisively, 'we're leaving. If you want to stay with your gigolo you can, but you'll be paying the bill, not us.'

We moved to another table and Mrs Sidebottom eventually joined us, but only after we noticed the waiter insisting that she paid for the whisky. 'Well,' she said, 'it was only a bit of fun, like.' We stayed in the dry for as long as we dared, before looking for a bus back to Calpe, the trains having been cancelled because of the landslide. The walk from the bus to the apartment was in the usual, wind, rain, thunder and lightning. That trip to Benidorm was the highlight of our holiday but we never ventured as far again. We stayed put, picking up the hailstones as they bounced down and out from our feature fireplace. There was no need for us to water the geraniums on the balcony, and no need to disobey the order not to take the towels on the beach, nor to turn off the tap at night. In truth, we were glad to set off for home, but the

F/H/B's opening remark when he met me was not very funny, 'Cor,' he said, 'you're white as a hound's tooth. Nobody'd ever think you'd bin in the sun for a fortnight!'

Autumn (2)
'Tis All Accordin'...

Many of the folk who have often been just tourists to Exmoor decide to buy a little property and move down for keeps. We can understand their desire to live in God's own country; even the locals feel privileged to live on Exmoor, and, inevitably, there are some who feel envious of our lifestyle, but it most certainly would not suit their needs. After all, not everybody wants to be a hillbilly hitched together with baler cord in a place little changed from, some say, fifty years ago. They smilingly admit money plays a big part in their decision, and we tell them we're happy to assist anybody to redistribute their wealth. As we always say, there's no disgrace in being poor, it's just the inconvenience of it.

Not everyone loves Exmoor enough to sacrifice their suburban Range Rover with its tin of spray-on-mud, for a temperamental tractor spattered with genuine sheep's droppings. Nor do they fancy swapping a champagne flute for a mug of cider, or their trendy pub with exotic dancers for ones with antlers over the doors and, inside on the wall, portraits of huntsmen long since gone.

Not all ladies love Exmoor. Scrutinising the local newspaper for a chic beauty salon they can be forgiven for recoiling at the eye-catching advertisement that grabs them with the promise 'Best prices paid for fat cows, plain cows and maiden heifers!'

Not everybody who comes to Exmoor wishes to sacrifice their vital statistics to trout, venison, rabbit, pheasant and clotted cream, nor do they savour exchanging their swimming pool for a sheep-dip. Nor does every incoming young male have the same lustful desire for a muscled young woman with the obligatory whinny that can be heard three fields away. Neither does she crave somebody that might be unaware that sound travels faster than stags on the moor, but one who is still not prepared to disclose the family scandals to save her time finding out. We used to call them the Goat and Chicken Brigade when urban husbands traded their suits and ties for corduroys and indestructible socks and sold up their suburban semi for 'a little place in the country'. They had day-dreamed for years of leaving behind the trains, the buses, the flight-paths, the sheer routine of it all, for something better, a Good Life. They were yet to discover the countryside would substitute rats, foxes, ticks, endless rain and armies of free-loading relatives who homed in on their new, themed Laura Ashley bedrooms, bearing a bottle of blended Scotch and a pot plant in lieu of payment for a fortnight's holiday.

They found the work hard and Daddy could be forgiven, on a cold winter's morning when struggling to milk the goat with knobbly titties, a small wave of nostalgia for the 8.15am to town with his newspaper folded under his arm, the warm office, and conversations with colleagues, not punctuated with trumpeting bleats from a fidgety goat. Still they would struggle on, pioneers, they told themselves, doing it for the family. But the children, who were used to city parks and leisure centres, were often openly resentful of their new rural surroundings, wrenching their eyes intermittently from the telly to whine there was nothing to do and they missed their friends. Their new pony would be saddled on Sunday afternoons for the family outing around the lanes, with the children, between tantrums, taking it in turn to ride and the goat trotting alongside, stinking, because, Mummy said, this is what people do in the country. Mummy was settling; she had a kitchen with an Aga and next week she would join the W.I. Daddy had reservations. Worrying that they had over-estimated their income, his target of five eggs per hen per week was already in arrears, the kitchen tap was spewing worms in what looked like gravy, and even with proper water he had not had a decent cup of tea since they started on the goat's milk.

Five years later (or less) would all too often see the end of the dream and a return to suburbia in a little terraced house with a parking space and Daddy back with his old firm on a guaranteed monthly salary and Tesco's just round the corner.

Ten years on sees a new breed of immigrant filtering into the West Country. They still snap up farms, rectories and even old manor houses, but this time round it is less about the Good Life and more about image and a country address. Couples stick with their own jobs, commuting, each in their own company car, covering hundreds of miles in three or four days before returning home to finish their week on computers.

They arrive, initially, in their jointly-owned third car, often towing a matching horse trailer containing an unmanageable thoroughbred ('His daddy won at Kempton') and a couple of Boxers who have never seen a sheep. They have not anticipated the darkness of the countryside and lose no time installing sensor light, beams and spotlights and even surveillance cameras, which only serve to feed the locals' endemic curiosity as to where these folk have come from and the sort of company they might be expecting at dead of night.

Improvements are high on their list of priorities and local trades people, who eagerly anticipate a redistribution of wealth, are often overlooked in favour of imported 'no planning permission, no questions asked', cowboy builders. A carpenter and plasterer were once, famously, shipped in from Sweden to totally about-turn an old farmhouse into an ultra-modern Swedish residence. Their employers probably lumped the Swede with us natives in the foreign language brigade.

For executives used to making snap decisions it must be an irritating time-waster attempting to extract a single scrap of information from a local, even if only a 'yes' or 'no' is at stake. Given that they can hardly expect a cultural exchange, they may be surprised to find that old-fashioned etiquette is alive and thriving in the country, and courtesies, along with the weather, are paramount before a native can even consider taking on board any questions. The crunch finally comes when the check cap is slowly removed and the head thoughtfully scratched before the standard, 'Well, 'tis all according' is enunciated.

At this stage, understandably, some incomers lose their cool and run screaming across the fields, but others, of a more placid turn of mind, soldier on, sensing that tact and diplomacy and a few hours to spare might be a worthwhile investment in their new lifestyle. They, in turn, are expected to feed us locals good information; snippets of the bits they are prepared to impart only whet the taste buds of those of us who are interested, and, not to put too fine a point on it, just plain curious. Information tends to creep out from properties as though bugged for sound into a loudhailer in Dulverton square. How else would folk know about the newcomer who every morning leapt out of bed, flung back the curtains and gazed at the view for ten seconds, then yelled, 'This was worth fighting for!' before jumping back under the covers. Or about the old farmer who was told by his doctor he must only do light jobs, and was reported to be sitting up in bed picking a chicken. Conversation-wise it is better for the new folk to plunge straight in, like the lady who announced, 'I'm here to celebrate burying my third husband!', though perhaps not a good idea for the chap who bragged about being an East-End gangster when, in fact, he only drove the getaway car. Events have a funny way of coming to light in the country, and come to light they will, because it must be near impossible to live any kind of double life under such scrutiny. Half-truths are also suspect, as with one neighbour, an ex-Navy man who used to go away for several weeks at a time, telling us that his current job was captain of a cruiser, and we all pictured him in his white dinner jacket entertaining at the captain's cocktail party as they cruised the blue Aegean. Nothing of the sort. It transpired, on one of our red-hot newsflashes, that the cruiser he commanded carted sewage out of Southend, thus earning him the nickname locally of Captain Crap.

As long as folk remember on Exmoor it's not WHO you are, but WHAT you are that counts, they should find no problem integrating. It also helps to be able to take the scandals that ricochet back and forth across the moor, gathering momentum with every mile, as with Patricia when she told me she had decided to go away for a couple of weeks to Almeria on a painting holiday. Auntie Dolly and Auntie Julie buttonholed me a few days later, saying they had heard Patricia would be going to America on a painting holiday.

'I think 'tis Almeria, in Spain,' I told them.

'No, no, 'tis America,' they declared, adamant. Then Seemingly turned up with, 'What's think about our new neighbour going off to America with a painter?' It's not surprising news on Exmoor is picked at with all the vigour of a buzzard picking on a dead sheep. Patricia had a sense of humour and could see the funny side of escalating scandal, but quickly reverted back to what the F/H/B called her 'bettermost' attitude.

'Just tell everyone I'm going to Almeria with a friend.' Then, sotto voce, 'She looks like someone's cook from the back, but knows Indian princes!'

A feature of autumn on Exmoor is the jumble sales, known collectively as Arrods. People are often known to give a bin-bagful of unwanted clothes to an Arrods, and come away with a further three bags full of somebody else's unwanted garments. It's not just the womenfolk who are hooked; Arrods can be just as addictive to husbands. One told me that he tried hard to give them up, but sank into depression on jumble days and had to revert back to his bad old ways. Some of the volunteer sales ladies would do credit to designer boutiques, such is their enthusiasm. I remember dubiously looking at a jacket at Arrods, a nice jacket and the right size, but I was dubious because I am ever mindful of the F/H/B's words.

'A bargain's never a bargain unless you really need it.'

But the sales lady was not one to give up without a fight. 'This jacket,' she told me, 'this jacket in lovat green with original stags-horn buttons, is in pristine condition.' She then leaned across the pile of jumble and lowered her voice conspiratorially, 'This jacket' – a dramatic pause – 'was the property of a concert pianist.'

'Who then?' I wanted to know. 'I'm not at liberty to say,' responded the assistant primly. 'But at this price it has to be a bargain.' I was hooked, I handed over fifty pence and the deal was clinched.

Sales on Exmoor operate at varying levels, from the pile 'em high jumble in the village hall to the more up-market table-top sale or charity nearly-new sales in private homes with £5 admission to include a slap-up lunch of smoked salmon, fresh fruit and cream and a glass of chilled wine. A Christian Dior suit was bought by Patricia for £8, a top price at any Arrods event. It was a quite hideous shade of mustard, but she screamed with delight, uncaring that the previous owner was a lady of more obvious generous proportions.

'That's not a problem,' she said, 'I shall cut down the skirt and carry the jacket over my arm with the label on the outside!'

It is a source of wonder to us locals that townspeople tend to dispose of their clothes long before they fall to pieces. Two neighbours were said to have actually argued over an expensive striped bodywarmer whilst it was still on its owner's back, but the dispute was solved for them one cold winter's day when they spotted the coveted garment strapped round a hairless goat who used the lane outside like a catwalk to parade it.

Not all gifts to Arrods are donated in a spirit of generosity; some garments are superfluous to requirements on account of being plain useless. One lady parted with five pence for a swimsuit only to find she ran into the sea a size-ten nymph and emerged pregnant after it filled with water.

It matters not that we are all wearing one another's clothes, change and interchange is the name of the game. One lady, crossing the square in Dulverton, was surprised to see a stranger waving to her from the other side.

'I'm sorry I don't recognise you,' said the first lady as they passed. 'No we've never met,' answered the second lady. 'But you are wearing my dress and I was waving to it!' Which just goes to show that shopping at Arrods is not only cheap, it can be very cheerful. And it makes a change from Lord Carnarvon's livery with two corn bags tied together with baler cord. I know that most of my clothes come from jumble sales, and I'm glad to wear them when I drive around to give talks. I always used to go in my old pig wagon before it collapsed and died, to deliver what the F/H/B termed Instantly Forgettable Rubbish. Although we called it the pig wagon, its main use was transporting sheep from field to field, and it stank accordingly, and it transferred to me when I donned my best clothes and drove to meetings. It called for a perfume strong enough to dowse the sheep, and my favourite lily-of-the-valley came nowhere near to that, so stronger measures were called for and I experimented until I found the killer perfume that filled the bill. Sometimes I see it advertised in the commercials on TV and wonder if I might not qualify for a free bottle if I offered to advertise its qualities; after all, nothing stinks quite like sheep.

At meetings I sometimes get to sit through the minutes of the previous month, and I often hear myself being discussed. Once they wondered where on earth they were going to scratch up the money to pay me as they only had £3 in the bank and another time, when I closed the season for a certain club, they had all agreed that when they reopened their new season they really must strive for a far higher class of speaker! Another time I filled in when the speaker who was booked was stricken with illness, and I gathered from the jolly little lady treasurer's words that she must have been not only a local speaker with no travelling expenses, but also a charity speaker with no fee.

'Anything to pay, anything to pay?' chanted the treasurer. As I was nearly 80 miles from home there most certainly were travelling expenses, plus my small (ish) fee. The little treasurer lady obviously thought I was not worth it because she enquired, incredulously, 'Will you be wanting ALL of it?' to which I had to answer in the affirmative. She looked horrified. 'Oh,' she said, as though it hurt, ''t'll mean another jumble sale!'

I once joined a lecture agency, and they sent me their rules. Never arrive late, never take along a friend for a free meal, always wear your best, and the added rule that I thought they put in for a joke, never arrive drunk. It was not a joke, they told me; some of the gentlemen speakers took fright at the thought of squaring up to vast numbers of ladies at luncheon clubs and resorted to a few snifters too many. They then, reported the agency, lost their notes – lost their glasses – it went from bad to worse, to mind-boggling.

Navigation never being my strong suit, I've spent a good many hours zooming around trying to find my way, and in so doing have met scores of interesting folk. I was heartened to meet a girl on a train who drove for Rolls-Royce who said she was constantly lost and driving down one-way streets. The difference was everyone gave way to her in her Rolls whilst I always was the one to back up in my pig van. One village hall I went to was obviously the wrong one because I opened the door to a room full of blue smoke and men in shirtsleeves playing billiards. Everything stopped, and they all looked at me.

'Oh,' I said, 'I can see I'm in the wrong place – I'm looking for the Women's Institute.'

A spokesman stepped from the crowd. ''Tis just round the corner, me dear,' he said, 'but why don't you stop along wi'us – you'd have a lot more fun!'

Perhaps the best summary of my talks came in a thank-you speech from a lady in Portsmouth – a summary of my life, in fact, when she said, 'And next month, ladies, in complete contrast to Norma Huxtable, we shall be having an afternoon of culture!'

Never mind – it's very jolly being a peasant, with or without culture...

◇◇◆◇◇